Bloom's Modern Critical Views

Modern Critical Views

AMY TAN

Edited and with an introduction by
Harold Bloom
Sterling Professor of the Humanities
Yale University

CHELSEA HOUSE PUBLISHERS
Philadelphia

© 2000, 2001, 2003 by Chelsea House Publishers,
a subsidiary of Haights Cross Communications.

Introduction © 2000 by Harold Bloom

Printed and bound in the United States of America

10   9   8   7   6   5   4

∞ The paper used in this publication meets the minimum
requirements of the American National Standard for
Permanence of Paper for Printed Library Materials,
Z39.48-1984

Library of Congress Cataloging-in-Publication Data

Amy Tan / edited with an introduction by Harold Bloom.
        p. cm—(Modern critical views)
    Includes bibliographical references and index.
    ISBN 0-7910-5658-9 (hc : alk. paper)
        1. Tan, Amy—Criticism and interpretation.   2. Women
and literature—United States—History—20th Century.
3. Chinese American women in literature.   4. Chinese
Americans in literature.   I. Bloom, Harold.   II. Series.
PS3570. A48 Z52   2000
813'.54—dc21
                                        99-051823
                                           CIP

Contributing Editor: Tenley Williams

Contents

Editor's Note

My Introduction centers upon "Two Kinds," excerpted from Amy Tan's best-known book, *The Joy Luck Club*.

Malini Johar Schueller compares Tan with Maxine Hong Kingston and finds in both a strong resistance to being marginalized, while Walter Shear sees Tan as placing a particular emphasis upon Chinese cultural identity as a healing element in the ruptures of family tradition brought about by emigration.

Marina Heung discovers in *The Joy Luck Club* a transformation from a mother-daughter text to a sister-text, after which Ben Xu meditates upon the dynamics of memory in Tan's first book.

Stephen Souris invokes the dialogical poetics of Bakhtin to explore agreement and disagreement in Tan, while Victoria Chen centers upon problems of language.

An interview with Amy Tan shows her awareness of the dangers of serving as a role model, after which Wendy Ho offers insights for teaching Tan.

The Hundred Secret Senses, a novel of the Taiping Rebellion, is surveyed by E. D. Huntley, while Yuan Yuan concludes this volume with another comparison of Tan and Kingston as pioneers of Chinese-American literary identity.

I am grateful to Tenley Williams for her assistance in editing this volume.

Introduction

I've written about Amy Tan's "Two Kinds" before, and return to it in this rather brief Introduction because it is a kind of paradigm-passage in what is still a very early phase of an emerging Chinese-American literature. The passage haunts me because it could fit equally well into the early Jewish-American literature of my youth, two-thirds of a century ago.

> She yanked me by the arm, pulled me off the floor, snapped off the TV. She was frighteningly strong, half pulling, half carrying me toward the piano as I kicked the throw rugs under my feet. She lifted me up and onto the hard bench. I was sobbing by now, looking at her bitterly. Her chest was heaving even more and her mouth was open, smiling crazily as if she were pleased I was crying.
>
> "You want me to be someone I'm not!" I sobbed. "I'll never be the kind of daughter you want me to be!"
>
> "Only two kinds of daughters," she shouted in Chinese. "Those who are obedient and those who follow their own mind! Only one kind of daughter can live in this house. Obedient daughter!"
>
> "Then I wish I wasn't your daughter. I wish you weren't my mother," I shouted. As I said these things I got scared. I felt like worms and toads and slimy things were crawling out of my chest, but it also felt good, as if this awful side of me had surfaced, at last.
>
> "Too late to change this," said my mother shrilly.
>
> And I could sense her anger rising to its breaking point. I wanted to see it spill over. And that's when I remembered the babies she had lost in China, the ones we never talked about.

"Then I wish I'd never been born!" I shouted. "I wish I were dead! Like them."

It was if I had said the magic words, Alakazam!—and her face went blank, her mouth closed, her arms went slack, and she backed out of the room, stunned, as if she were blowing away like a small brown leaf, thin, brittle, lifeless.

This has the power of simplicity and of universality, though its style is a touch inadequate to its anguish. "Two Kinds" has the irony, as a title, of meaning also two worlds, China and the United States. The daughter, understandably in flight from a love so possessive that it could destroy, is also obsessed by an unwarranted yet inevitable guilt. And yet she must rebel, since the musical genius that her mother demands is simply not there. I remember acquaintances of my own childhood, in the later 1930's in the East Bronx, who suffered agonies of enforced violin lessons, as though each one of them could revive the musical tradition of Jewish Odessa. I still bless my long-dead mother for letting me alone, so that I could sit on the floor in a corner to read endlessly, which is all that I have ever wanted to do.

Tan's mother backs away "like a small brown leaf, thin, brittle, lifeless," more a ghost than a person. The image again is universal, being as much Homeric and Virgilian as Chinese. Amy Tan is still young enough to get beyond *The Joy Luck Club*, though she has not yet done so. Whatever the future course of her work will be, she at least has joined Maxine Hong Kingston in breaking a new road, doubtless at considerable inner cost.

MALINI JOHAR SCHUELLER

Theorizing Ethnicity and Subjectivity: Maxine Hong Kingston's Tripmaster Monkey and Amy Tan's The Joy Luck Club

When women of color began to voice their estrangement from the theories and concerns of white feminists, they dramatized the fact that they had for too long been the objects of representation. The task of these women was twofold: that of deconstructing the male/female binary opposition of white feminism by interjecting concerns of race, colonialism, and imperialism; and that of constructing theories of "identity" (and I use the term deliberately with caution) for women of color. Understandably, it was the deconstructive project that was (and is being) first undertaken with great energy. To mention only a few critics, there were those like Gayatri Spivak who deconstructed liberal feminist literary criticism and revealed its investment in the emancipation of white women alone; women like bell hooks revealed the concerns of Euro-American feminism to be restricted to those of middle-class white women; critics such as Valerie Amos and Pratibha Parmar questioned the politics of feminists who viewed imperialism as having been historically progressive for Third World women. However, the task of construction has been much more complicated and fraught with ambivalences. On the one hand, women of color have had to emphasize their particular concerns, their differences from ideologies of universal womanhood—whether Anglo-American or French—while on the other hand they have been concerned about the problems of espousing a racial/ethnic

From *Genders* 15 (Winter 1992). © 1992 by the University of Texas Press.

essence. The concern with essentialism in feminist debates today, in other words, is also a major concern in theoretical discussions of ethnicity as well as in fictional works of women of color. Here, I wish to examine the task of construction in discussions of ethnicity and show how a focus on representation and the discursivity of identity offers possible alternatives to the notion of a racial/ethnic essence. I argue that such a focus is not restricted to theory but is, in fact, a major concern in two recent texts by Chinese-American women writers: *Tripmaster Monkey* by Maxine Hong Kingston and *The Joy Luck Club* by Amy Tan.

Some of the difficulties associated with constructing ethnicity in the context of a posthumanistic consciousness are evident in Lisa Lowe's insightful essay on the Asian-American subject. Lowe stresses the heterogeneity of Asian-American culture in order ultimately to "disrupt the current hegemonic relationship between 'dominant' and 'minority' positions." Yet it is necessary, Lowe further acknowledges, to keep the concept of ethnic identity "for the purpose of contesting and disrupting the discourses that exclude Asian American(s)." To completely give up the model of oppression in formulations of ethnicity is to give up too much. Indeed the most problematic use to which ethnicity has been put has been the one that depoliticizes the term, dissociates it from marginalization and oppression, and opposes it to a supposedly fixed concept of race. To this camp belong Anglo-American critics who invoke the ideology of the melting pot and, without any sensitivity to relations of power and dominance, see a similarity among all "ethnic" groups—Irish-American, Italian-American, African-American. Of course one only has to glance at the centuries of hysteria about racial miscegenation in the United States to see the problems in invoking such similarities. Such a concept of ethnicity is of little use to women of color and must, indeed, be regarded with suspicion. The question seems to be the use to which ethnic definitions are put. There needs to be a healthy suspicion of definitions because it is precisely by using the strategy of restrictive definition and hierarchical binary opposition that the dominant culture has oppressed marginal groups. But this also does not mean that there is no political importance in appropriating the second term in the hierarchy and empowering it in slogans such as "black is beautiful." However, such slogans are empowering precisely because they question the hierarchy; what is empowering is the act of appropriation. "Black is beautiful" expresses a political solidarity but does not suggest that there is an essential "blackness" to be empowered. The difficult task for women of color, then, is to articulate a politics of resistance and difference without resorting to purely definitional conceptions of ethnic identity.

The first step toward such a construction is to think of ethnicity not simply as essence but as representation, as something linguistically constructed. (After all, it is representations such as the black rapist, the duplicitous Asian, or the passive Asian woman that are used to dominate and suppress minorities.) While constructions of subjectivity by liberal white feminists have typically relied on notions of the singular, autonomous self, women of color have typically stressed collective and social subjectivities. Marxist theorists of language and subjectivity have similarly rejected the isolated, autonomous psyche of Freudian psychology for a conception of the psyche as a social and discursive entity. The psyche, according to Bakhtin, "enjoys extraterritorial status . . . [as] a social entity." Experience is available to this psyche not in some immediate fashion but through a network of signs, most importantly, language. "Not only can experience be outwardly expressed through the agency of the sign . . . but also aside from this outward expression (for others), experience exists even for the person undergoing it only in the material of signs. Outside that material there is no experience as such." The importance of a discursive notion of self in thinking about ethnicity is that it provides a powerful indictment of the idea of an essential, abstract biological self beyond language and society. It is a way of retaining the concept of identity, but as a social construct, constantly reformulated and reformulating itself through language. It is also a way of resisting essentialist definitions of ethnicity.

In *Tripmaster Monkey* and *The Joy Luck Club*, Kingston and Tan affirm a politics of resistance and difference and thematize the construction of a Chinese-American identity. Interestingly, representation plays a key role in the formation of ethnic identity in both works. Both works also emphasize the socially constructed, discursive nature of gender and ethnic identity. Kingston uses the discursivity of ethnic identity to completely subvert the idea of cultural origins while Tan uses discursivity to show how cultural origins are multiple and complex. In very different ways, the two works raise questions about ethnicity, identity, and difference which are crucial to the concerns of women of color.

Tripmaster Monkey is about the hopes, anxieties, fears, and angers of Wittman Ah Sing—first-generation Chinese-American, Berkeley graduate, fired retail employee, cynical lover, long-haired peacenik, passionate playwright—as he walks the streets of San Francisco reflecting on his place in American society and reading Rilke aloud to passengers on a Bay Area bus. It ends with Wittman staging a play for his Chinese-American audience and using the theater as a public forum to comment on the pathologizing of Chinese as exotic. In *The Woman Warrior* Kingston wrote polemically as a Chinese-American woman battling an oppressive white male culture and also deconstructed hierarchical oppositions between Chinese and American, male and female. In *Tripmaster Monkey* Kingston further problematizes and subverts restrictive ethnic definitions by emphasizing the complex processes of representation and interpretation involved in the formulation of any such definition.

In a sense, the entire novel is an extended meditation on representation. Kingston emphasizes the marginalization of people of color by rewriting the "classic" texts of white American writers. Her hero, named Wittman by his actor father, is the latter-day incarnation of the poet of democracy and diversity, the supremely American poet who embraces the high and the low, the bleeding slave and the Indian. But Kingston, by presenting her novel as a modern "Song of Myself," compellingly confronts us with the fact that the prerogative to speak to and embody all America has always been a white male one: "'Call me Ishmael.' See? You pictured a white guy, didn't you? If Ishmael were described—ochery ecru amber umber skin—you picture a *tan* white guy. Wittman wanted to spoil all those stories coming out of and set in New England Back East—to blacken and to yellow Bill, Brooke, and Annie. A new rule for the imagination: The common man has Chinese looks. From now on, whenever you read about those people with no surnames, color them with black skin or Yellow skin."

Kingston's appropriation of *Moby Dick*, the classic American epic, is an act of empowerment through which the Chinese Other can have a voice in America. And just as Kingston examines the hegemony of white American culture through its literary representation, thus emphasizing the discursivity of American identity, she similarly emphasizes the constructed nature of Chinese ethnic identity. Although Wittman despises the "Oriental Tea Garden" variety of exoticism, his own perceptions of Chinese people are influenced by the representations of Chinese in American popular culture. Walking the streets of San Francisco, Wittman sees "a Chinese dude from China, hands clasped behind, bow-legged, loose-seated, out on a stroll—that walk they do in kung fu movies when they are full of contentment on a sunny day." Interestingly, this is a description of a "Fresh Off the Boats" immigrant Chinese, one who should logically be the repository of an "original" culture. Kingston, however, suggests that the very idea of what an ethnic essence is comes out of popular representations. What Wittman is presented with, through the narrating voice, is both the nominal "original" and the second-hand represented simultaneously. Representation and reality, the socially constructed stereotypical and the experiential are inseparably mixed in Wittman's perceptions of ethnic difference.

It is, therefore, extremely significant that Kingston chooses the profession of playwright for her hero. Wittman is agonizingly conscious of the different social roles he plays and keeps a running narrative of the play he is currently writing. He constantly undermines and subverts the narrow roles assigned to Chinese people in American culture. Instead of conforming to the demure and decorous look of Ivy League Chinese, Wittman flaunts his long-haired hippie look. To the officer at the unemployment office who attempts to classify him as a potential retail manager, as his last job indicates, he insists he be listed as a playwright. As his friend Nanci, the aspiring actress, constantly finds, being accepted in America means playing certain ethnic roles. At her auditions, Nanci is told to "act more Oriental." "You don't sound the way you look. You don't look the way you talk." Angered by the straitjacketing Chinese are faced with, Wittman vows to wrest the theater back for the Chinese.

Wittman's stage production literally becomes an arena for alternative enactments of ethnicity. The cast of characters, which includes nearly all the characters in the book, participate in Wittman's play based on the epic Chinese *Romance of the Three Kingdoms*. But these Chinese-Americans, despite the mediation of the play and Wittman's attempts to subvert narrow racial definitions, are still subject to essentialist racial interpretation. Reviews of the play praise it as "East meets West," "sweet and sour," and "singing rice," much in the same manner as many of the reviews of Kingston's own works. Kingston does not suggest that the Chinese are simply the passive objects of Western definition. Like the natives who, in a colonial situation, internalize the norms and values of colonizers, the Chinese, too, see themselves through the eyes of their American viewers and enthusiastically applaud the reviews. Angered by the inability of the Chinese to perceive their own pathologizing, Wittman uses the stage to harangue his audience: "We're about as exotic as shit. Nobody special here. No sweet-and-sour shit. No exotic chop suey shit. So this variety show had too much motley; they didn't have to call it 'chop suey vaudeville' . . . Do I have to explain why 'exotic' pisses me off, and 'not exotic' pisses me off? They've got us in a bag, which we aren't punching our way out of." Giving voice to the culturally marginalized is thus not a question of proclaiming the primacy of certain ethnic values over others—indeed, Kingston has her protagonist constantly scoff at what are perceived as particularly "Chinese" traits—but rather that of adopting a conscious political position of resistance to the oppressive definitions of the dominant culture. Indeed, Kingston makes her protagonist challenge these definitions by taking them seriously at the literal level and thus revealing the racial ideologies such definitions seek to hide. As Wittman shouts to his audience: "I'm common ordinary. Plain black sweater. Blue jeans. Tennis shoes ordinaire. Clean soo mun shaven. What's so exotic?"

It is also important to emphasize that this resistance to definition is part of a politics of difference and not a coded longing to be part of a common "American" humanity. Kingston's works have too often been misread as exactly that. *The Woman Warrior*, for example, has been read as an attempt of the narrator to escape from Chinese restriction to American freedom. Similarly Wittman's politics in *Tripmaster Monkey* have been seen as "his identification with the ideals of the melting pot." But the ideology of the melting pot is a stance of pluralism and traditional liberal humanism. Humanism argues that at the end of all theorizing we are left with an essential humanity, a metaphysical identity which it is the purpose of activism to affirm and defend. The assumption is that although there are different social groups, these groups are positioned in relations of democratic equality and any consensual ideology emerges from an equal participation by all groups. Such an assumption denies the existence of class structure and the very real inequalities of power and position that all marginalized groups, particularly women of color, are subject to. Kingston, too, is conscious of the disempowerment of Chinese-Americans and is determined not to subsume their interests under the hegemony of a unified melting pot ideology. When Wittman rails about having "failed . . . to burst through their Kipling" and argues that in his play "there is no East. . . . West is meeting West," he ruptures the hierarchical division which views the East as aberrance and challenges his American viewers to nurture a society of radical differences. Instead of accepting the definitions of the dominant culture, Wittman argues for a strategic and political group identity. Knowing full well that the term "American" is used "interchangeably with 'white,'" Wittman suggests that the Chinese politicize their identity. "It's our fault they call us gook and chinky chinaman," says Wittman. "We've been here all this time, before Columbus, and haven't named ourselves. Look at the Blacks beautifully defining themselves."

Kingston's conception of social difference and her view of ethnicity as a represented, social construct are both intimately related to her rejection of the stable and unified subject on which both humanist and essentialist racial visions depend. The loquacious and energetic hero of *Tripmaster Monkey*, unlike the sage after whom he is named, is not the transcendent poet who can rise above the social-material world into visions of spiritual unity but the person of this world whose identity is constituted by Otherness and is always changing. *Tripmaster Monkey* begins with a vision of Wittman's body scattered into fragments as he laconically contemplates suicide much in the manner of Hart Crane's speaker in *The Bridge*. Throughout the novel, Wittman enacts changes of character and identity. Accosted on the bus by a Chinese woman who stereotypes him as the quiet Asian science whiz,

Wittman plays the role to fit the part:

> "I don't know what you say," says Wittman. Know like no, like
> brain. "I major in engineer."
>   "Where do you study engineering?"
>   "Ha-ah." He made a noise like a samurai doing a me-ay,
> or an old Chinese guy who smokes too much.

At other times, Wittman talks rap, wishes the Chinese had their own jazz and blues, and tries to appropriate the demeanor of the "heroic Black man" when he hears people at a restaurant cracking "chink joke[s]." Wittman thrives on being multifaceted, on driving his car like "an international student from a developing country" or like an "Oakie." At Colt Tower he plays at getting married to a white girl, Tana, by a man who is possibly a minister, while the production of his play turns into a marriage celebration as the Chinese actor-audience shower rice on the couple. Life and art, play and reality, Kingston suggests, are not easily demarcated.

Just as Kingston sees ethnicity and subjectivity as constituted by representation and social construction, she also views gender as a social construct and a site of difference. In *The Woman Warrior* Kingston had emphasized the variability of femininity and deconstructed oppositions between male and female, American and Chinese. Kingston "violate[d] the law of opposition, making gender dichotomies proliferate into unresolved gender differences." In *Tripmaster Monkey* she deliberately undermines any notion of an essential, singular female identity by making Wittman her central character and thus challenging easy experiential identification. At the same time, Kingston makes clear that gender boundaries are always constructed. It is significant that PoPo, the grandmother who has partly raised Wittman and to whom he is emotionally attached, calls him "honey girl" and "Wit Man." And the guise in which Wittman most frequently appears subverts traditional gender and ethnic dichotomies. Wittman is the modern-day reincarnation of Monkey King, the mythological trickster figure from Wu Cheng-en's sixteenth-century novel *The Pilgrimage to the West*. As a figure of Chinese mythology the monkey is firmly anchored within the culture, yet subject to change. The monkey breaks taboos, is punished by the gods, but manages to escape difficult situations through trickery. He goes along with the monk on a pilgrimage to get Buddhist scriptures, but he demonstrates the real impracticality of Buddhist pacifism in fighting with devils. The monk is spiritual, devout, and unquestioning; the monkey is earthly, appetitive, sensual, and changing. Unlike the monk, the monkey can change into different forms and can see through the various guises taken on by devils.

Kingston's use of the monkey as the figure for the ethnic subject is an affirmation of difference and resistance. Like the Afro-American signifying monkey who dwells in the margins of discourse and who challenges the dominant culture by multiple voicings, Kingston's Chinese-American Monkey King speaks for the people of Chinatown but refuses a singular ethnic discourse. As a feminist of color it is important for Kingston to reject ethnic discourses which celebrate a singular Chinese identity. Such discourses belong to the language of patriarchal absolutism that women of color need to cast off. Kingston's decision to use a male protagonist instead of dealing directly with the experiences of women (as she did in *The Woman Warrior*) also suggests her determination to dissociate the concerns of women from simple biodeterminism alone. Kingston herself has suggested that the "omniscient narrator in *Tripmaster Monkey* is a Chinese American woman; she's Kwan Yin (the Goddess of Mercy) and she's me." It is not as if Kingston associates her male protagonist with more "universal" values. Instead, she uses him to suggest the problems with gender dichotomies that equate maleness with singularity and universality and thus uses the occasion of the male protagonist to subvert gender oppositions much like she did in *The Woman Warrior*. The same is the case with ethnicity. If there is no "real" China or Chinese-American culture to valorize, there is no "real" Americanism that immigrants need espouse. Indeed, the striking feature of the book is that although it is so concerned with immigrant experience and the politics of assimilation, there is no Oedipal quest structure, the end of which is the attainment of a certain kind of ethnicity. There is, instead, a celebration of multiple enactments of ethnicity. Through Wittman, Kingston shows how ethnic identity as a shifting, constantly reformulated concept, related to an "origin" only through linguistic representations and fictions, is, in fact, empowering.

In contrast to *Tripmaster Monkey*, Amy Tan's *The Joy Luck Club* deals explicitly with the experiences of Chinese-American women and their acculturation in a new environment. The narrative centers around the lives of four Mandarin-speaking Chinese immigrant mothers in San Francisco who have formed a mah-jongg group called the Joy Luck Club and the American-born daughters of these mothers. The narrative unfolds through the four different mother-daughter narrators telling the stories of their lives. Tan places a decided emphasis on mother-daughter relationships, and much of the work can be seen as a celebration of values such as nurturance and connectedness that have been seen by many feminists to characterize women as opposed to male values such as separation and autonomy. But Tan ensures that her work cannot simply be recuperated as an ahistorical feminism without attention to the particular status of women of color within universalist feminism. Like Kingston who presents ethnicity as a construct, Tan presents Chinese-American women's identity as resistance by appropriating (and thus questioning) the rhetoric of universalist feminism.

In order to appreciate Tan's appropriation, we need to consider the representations of women of color when they are the objects of feminist analysis. Aihwa Ong explains the dynamics of these representations as follows: "By portraying women in non-Western societies as identical and interchangeable, and more exploited than women in dominant capitalist societies, liberal and socialist feminists alike encode a belief in their own cultural superiority. . . . Studies on women in post-1949 China inevitably discuss how they are doubly exploited by the peasant family and by the socialist patriarchy." Within white American culture the dichotomies between Western and Asian women are clearly seen as those between activity and passivity, freedom and restraint, independence and submission. Tan is aware of these dichotomies and attempts to undermine the imperialism within universalist feminism. In *The Joy Luck Club* Tan polemically records the marginalization and disempowerment of all women within patriarchal institutions—whether in China or America. While wives within the traditional Chinese family are taught to find satisfaction in waiting on their husbands and their families, in America the mass media insidiously reinforces the same subservience. As Lindo Jong, one of the Chinese mothers, reflects, "I hurt so much I didn't feel any difference. What was happier than seeing everybody gobble down the shiny mushrooms and bamboo shoots I had helped prepare that day? . . . How much happier could I be after seeing Tyan-yu eat a whole bowl of noodles without complaining about its taste or my looks? It's like those ladies you see on American TV these days, the ones who are so happy they have washed out a stain so the clothes look better than new." Tan's subversion of the distinction between the progressive (Euro-American) woman and the traditional Asian woman is radical here. Lindo Jong, the woman who was married at the age of eight and sent to live with her husband's family at the age of twelve, is not only equated with the (ostensibly) free American woman but is also given the power to interpret her Western counterpart. Similarly, Tan uses another Chinese immigrant mother to voice the idea of the disempowerment of women across cultures and generations. Reflecting on the despair of her American-born daughter over an impending divorce, An-Mei Hsu concludes: "If she doesn't speak, she is making a choice. . . . I know this, because I was raised the Chinese way: I was taught to desire nothing. . . . And even though I taught my daughter the opposite, she still came out the same way! Maybe it was because she was born to me and she was born a girl. And I was born to my mother and I was born to be a girl. All of us are like stairs, one step after another, going up and down, but all going the same way." Tan's formulation of a common oppression shared by what is traditionally perceived as Chinese-raised and American-raised women again subverts East-West cultural dichotomies. Tan carefully relies upon and upsets these hierarchical cultural expectations. "Because I was raised the Chinese way" in the above passage, for example, strategically reveals the imperialist racial context within which such casual formulations are taken as completely explanatory. In another instance Tan deconstructs the myth of American freedom. Male polygamy in China sanctions the mistreatment of women and their relegation to concubine status, the humiliation of which An-Mei Hsu's mother escapes only through suicide. However, in America, the ethnic woman is subject to dual disempowerment of ethnicity and gender. The seemingly lovable Irish husband of Ying-Ying St. Clair proudly imagines himself having "saved" his Chinese wife from some hideous, unimaginable life and passes this myth on to his daughter. In reality, as Ying-Ying reflects, she was "raised with riches he could not even imagine" and he had to wait for four years "like a dog in a butcher shop" before she consented to marry him. Once in America, St. Clair, in a sense, enslaves Ying-Ying. He crosses out Ying-Ying's Chinese name on her passport papers, names her Betty St. Clair, gives her a new birthdate, and insists she speak English. "So with him, she spoke in moods and gestures, looks and silences. . . . Words cannot come out. So my father put words in her mouth." The result: madness.

Just as Tan depicts a common oppression of women, she also depicts a resistance through maternal bonding and nurturing. The novel begins with the death of Suyan Woo, mother of Jing-Mei Woo and founder of the Joy Luck Club. A woman of incredible strength and moral courage, Suyan Woo started the Joy Luck Club, a mah-jongg group, during the Japanese invasion of China. Amidst the destruction and poverty caused by the invasion, the women decided to create an oasis of good cheer in which they pretended to be rich and carefree. The novel ends with Jing-Mei Woo going to China to meet her half-sisters, the two daughters Suyan Woo was forced to abandon during the invasion but which she never gave up trying to locate. Jing-Mei Woo's journey to China is thus a journey back to her mother, a retrieval of her memory into the present. "Together we look like our mother. Her same eyes, her same mouth, open in surprise to see, at last, her long-cherished wish." Throughout the book we see the intensity and power of mother-daughter bonds. An-Mei Hsu's mother literally tears off her flesh and offers it in sacrifice in an attempt to revive her dying mother; Rose-Hsu Jordan is able to demand her divorce rights by imaginative identification with her mother; and Jing-Mei Woo looks for the memory of her mother to help her understand the present.

And this female identity as defined through the mother-daughter bond is integrally linked to ethnic identity. As Amy Ling suggests, the lost mother is a trope for lost motherland. The return to the mother is also the return to cultural roots; separation from the mother is a separation from one's own cultural origins. Ying-Ying St. Clair's determination to bridge the separation between her daughter and herself is a synecdoche of the narratives of separation and togetherness that inform the text. "There is a part of her mind that is part of mine. . . . All her life I have watched her as though from another shore. And now I must tell her everything about my past. It is the only way to penetrate her skin and pull her to where she can be saved."

But Tan builds up the romantic concept of cultural origins and lost ethnic essence only in order to radically undermine and reconfigure the notion of an ethnic essence. The narrative of separation and return—symbolized by Jing-Mei Woo's return to China/mother—on the plot level is questioned by the rhetorical structure of the text which undercuts any notions of simple identification of origins or of a cultural "reality" easily available for access. The experiences of Chinese immigrants in America and their past lives in China are not documented by a seemingly objective narrator but by a series of participants narrating their extremely subjective experiences. Tan's decision to have several mothers and daughters telling their different stories reflects her awareness of ethnicity as a constantly shifting social construct and her commitment to community. The mothers and daughters tell their stories within the framework of the Joy Luck Club, the purpose of which is to keep alive a memory of the past and create a community. Each section of the novel actually creates a different version of femininity and ethnicity. While the first section of the novel emphasizes the loss of separation from mothers, the second emphasizes the competitiveness of the relationship. Thus we have An-Mei Hsu's mother, who determinedly, despite the curses of her family, takes her daughter to live with her even though she only has the status of concubine; we also have Jing-Mei Woo, the Chinese-American daughter who wishes to understand and unite with the memories of her dead mother. On the other hand, we have immigrant Chinese mothers who project their cultural anxieties on their daughters. Waverly Jong's mother, for instance, parades her daughter's chess trophies and lectures to her about winning tournaments while Suyan Woo tries unsuccessfully to create a musical child prodigy out of her unmusical daughter Jing-Mei Woo.

Further, Tan's construction of ethnic identity is not based on a vision of a stable and unchanging China that can be recalled at will. Although the theme of estrangement from, and unification with, cultural origins is integral to the work, these origins are multiple and discursive. Part of Tan's purpose in having four different Chinese-born mothers is to introduce different versions of China, neither of which is prioritized over the other. At the most obvious level, there are clear class differences among the mothers' experiences of China. Auntie Lin's family in China revels in consumerism, surrounding itself with color TV sets and remote controls; An-Mei Hsu's family, on the other hand, is awed at having a relative in the land of consumer goods. More importantly, for the American-born daughters, the Chinese past exists discursively, in language, through the stories told about it by their mothers. Ethnic origins, in other words, are always already complicated by representation. For An-Mei Hsu, a Chinese mother, for example, "China" is a mixture of memories of her mother's suicide and of peasant uprisings that she reads of in magazines from China, all of which have to be sorted out by her psychiatrist. The most interesting example of ethnic origins being based on multiple and changing representations is the history of the Joy Luck Club itself. Suyan Woo tells her daughter the history of the Joy Luck Club which she started in Kweilin, but the history changes with each retelling. Her daughter, who has heard the story many times, never thinks her mother's Kweilin story about the origins of the Joy Luck Club is "anything but a Chinese fairy tale. The endings always changed. Sometimes she said she used that worthless thousand-yuan note to buy a half-cup of rice. She turned that rice into a pot of porridge. . . . The story always grew and grew." In many ways, the club itself deconstructs traditionally perceived oppositions between history and fiction, the experiential and the discursive. The club is formed as a make-believe celebration of plenty during the devastation of Japanese occupation and thus has a fictive function. Yet the club survives as Suyan Woo's most "real" memory of the war period. The club is based on stories, "stories spilling out all over the place." The women tell each other stories about "good times in the past and good times yet to come," pretending each week is a new year, and this self-consciously fictive club becomes the basis for creating an immigrant community in California.

Similarly, Tan's mode of narration questions the very idea of historical context as something that can be retrieved through a recording of facts. Tan uses a dialogic mixture of myth, fantasy, reverie, and historical facts without demarcating any as more true than the other and thus questions the truth status of a national history. Within "true" stories of the Chinese past of immigrant mothers, stories of arranged marriages and Japanese occupation, there are affective images of mythical women like the Moon Lady and grotesque images of destructive mothers dismembering their daughters. The concept of a Chinese woman's identity, Tan suggests, is a discursive one. Similarly, the last section of the book, which includes four narratives of mothers and daughters coming to an understanding, is titled "Queen Mother of the Western Skies" and obviously invokes the figure of Queen Mother, the feminization of Buddha who appears (in White Lotus Buddhism) as the creator of mankind and the controller of time. The blend of myth and traditional historical storytelling that informs the narratives about China suggests that ethnic origins are always created and recreated in the complex process of social representation. To think of ethnicity as an essence is to fall prey to the fortune cookie syndrome, to create monologic definitions in order to manage differences. As An-Mei Hsu tells Lindo Jong about fortune cookies, "American people think Chinese people write these sayings." "But we never say such things!" I said. "These things don't make sense."

Tan's simultaneous use of the motif of the return to origins and her complication of these origins raises a matter of unquestionable importance for women of color. Is it desirable for a radical feminist politics to view femininity and ethnicity as ever-changing social constructs? Is it possible to demand and affect social change without the construction of a whole and unified subject? The answer to both those questions has to be a yes if only because the alternatives are so dangerous. As an example of the problems inherent in momentarily positing a singular ethnicity and femininity we can look, for a moment, at Tan's text. The last chapter of *The Joy Luck Club* presents an idealized moment of ethnic identity, set deliberately against the multiplicities of the rest of the novel. The chapter concerns Jing-Mei Woo's trip to China to meet her two half-sisters whom her mother was forced to abandon and who have been miraculously located by the members of the Joy Luck Club. The trope of the lost motherland and the lost mother become one here. Jing-Mei Woo feels herself "becoming" Chinese as the train crosses the border from Hong Kong. "Once you are born Chinese, you cannot help but feel and think Chinese. . . . It is in your blood." The entire chapter enacts a rhapsody of ethnic identity as Jing-Mei and her father meet old relatives and finally the two lost sisters. Here Jing-Mei Woo understands an ethnic identity that is beyond language: "And now I also see what part of me is Chinese. It is so obvious. It is my family. It is in our blood. After all these years, it can finally be let go." But while Tan celebrates this moment of ethnic wholeness, she is also aware of the problems that such essentialist concepts pose. Moments such as these deny the class differences between the tourist gazer and the ethnic subject and suggest an ethnic oneness that the text thus far has questioned. Tan therefore chooses to end her narrative not with this moment but with a commentary on it. The text ends with Jing-Mei and her sisters looking at a Polaroid photo of themselves that Jing-Mei's father has just taken, and with Jing-Mei recognizing her mother in the composite of the three sisters. Jing-Mei recognizes an ethnic identification but only through her active interpretation and by deliberately framing ethnic "subjects" in a momentary stasis beyond language.

Kingston and Tan succeed in creating a space for women of color to articulate themselves because they refuse to use definitional modes of locating gender and ethnic identity. Kingston presents a constructed and discursive ethnic identity by having her protagonist take on multiple roles and constantly enact versions of ethnicity, while Tan does so by presenting multiple representations of ethnic origins. The emphasis on the discursivity and contextuality of ethnic identity does not mean that Kingston and Tan are attempting to write from beyond ethnicity or that they are denying the importance of racial divisions in society. On the contrary, it attests to the determination of these women to use ethnicity as resistance, to articulate it in such a manner that it cannot be reduced to definitional criteria which have always been used to marginalize people of color.

WALTER SHEAR

Generational Differences and the Diaspora in The Joy Luck Club

Orville Schell's review of *The Joy Luck Club* for the *New York Times* emphasizes that those millions of Chinese who were part of the diaspora of World War II and the fighting that resulted in the triumph of the Communists were subsequently cut off from the mainland and after 1949 left to fend for themselves culturally. Though Schell is struck by the way this book renders the vulnerability of these Chinese women in America, the novel's structure in fact succeeds in manifesting not merely the individual psychic tragedies of those caught up in this history, but the enormous agony of a culture enmeshed in a transforming crisis. What each person's story conveys is the terror of a vulnerable human consciousness torn and rent in a culture's contortions; and although, like other Chinese-American books, this novel articulates "the urge to find a usable past" it is made up of a series of intense encounters in a kind of cultural lost and found.

The structure that presents this two-fold impression recalls works such as Sherwood Anderson's *Winesburg, Ohio*, Ernest Hemingway's *In Our Time*, and William Faulkner's *The Unvanquished*, books that feature distinct, individual narratives but that as a group simultaneously dramatize the panorama of a critical transition in cultural values. In *The Joy Luck Club* Tan organizes her material in terms of a generational contrast by segregating stories of mothers and their daughters. The separate story sections are

From *Critique* Vol. 34, No. 3 (Spring 1993). © 1993 by the Helen Dwight Reid Educational Foundation.

17

divided into four parts with mother figures telling two stories, mostly concerned with their past in pre-1949 China, and their daughters telling two stories, one about growing up and one about a current family situation. The exception to this pattern is Jing-mei Woo, the daughter of the founder of the Joy Luck Club, who narrates a story in each of the four sections and who adds additional continuity by narrating the first and last section. Though all these people, for the most part, know one another, few of the stories involve contacts with anyone outside the immediate family group. While the daughters' stories usually involve their mothers, the mothers' stories tend to feature a distinct life, involving rather rigid family experiences in old China and their current relationship to their American daughters. By using the perspectives of both mothers and daughters, Tan initially seems to solve what Linda Hunt, examining Maxine Hong Kingston, describes as a basic problem for a Chinese-American woman: "being simultaneously insider (a person who identifies strongly with her cultural group) and outsider (deviant and rebel against that tradition), she cannot figure out from which perspective to speak."

Nevertheless, just as in *The Woman Warrior*, the communication barrier here is a double one, that between generations and that created by the waning influence of an older culture and the burgeoning presence of another. Jing-mei announces in the first section: "My mother and I never really understood one another. We translated each other's meanings and I seemed to hear less than what was said, while my mother heard more." Generally, the daughters tend to perceive cultural blanks, the absence of clear and definite answers to the problems of family, whereas the mothers tend to fill in too much, often to provide those kinds of cultural answers and principles that seem to empower them to make strong domestic demands on their daughters. Thus, as in *Woman Warrior*, the object of "confrontation" for a daughter is often the mother, "the source of authority for her and the most single powerful influence from China."

The mothers tend to depict themselves as, in a broad sense, students learning about the social realities around them and using their experiences to come to conclusions about essential forms of character strength and weakness. For example, one of the mothers, An-mei Hsu, seems to see in her own mother's suicide how to use the world for her own advantage. She not only traces how her mother makes the Chinese cultural beliefs work for her—"suicide is the only way a woman can escape marriage and gain revenge, to come back as a ghost and scatter tea leaves and good fortune"—but also she realizes almost immediately the acute significance of the words of her mother who tells her "she [the mother] would rather kill her own weak spirit so she could give me a stronger one."

Ying-ying St. Clair claims, "I have always known a thing before it happens." Her daughter tends to confirm at least an ironic version of her mother's acquired powers by adding, "She sees only bad things that affect our family." In at least one case the mother's knowledge is a gift passed to the daughter: Waverly Jong opens her story by claiming, "I was six when my mother taught me the art of invisible strength. It was a strategy for winning arguments, respect from others, and eventually, though none of us knew it at the time, chess games." In the last case the knowledge apparently blossoms from the mother's folk saying, "Bite back your tongue," and although Waverly regards it as a secret of her success in chess, she herself is finally a victim of her mother's more authoritarian deployment of the tactic, as it suddenly takes the form of simply ignoring her.

As the last interaction demonstrates, there is nearly always some tension in the exchange between mother and daughter, between old China and the new American environment. Most often the focus is either on a mother, who figures out her world, or on the daughters, who seem caught in a sophisticated cultural trap, knowing possibilities rather than answers, puzzling over the realities that seem to be surrounding them and trying to find their place in what seems an ambivalent world. Strangely, given the common problems presented, there is little concern with peer communication among the daughters. Jing-mei explains, "Even though Lena and I are still friends, we have grown naturally cautious about telling each other too much. Still, what little we say to one another often comes back in another guise. It's the same old game, everybody talking in circles." This difficulty in communication may simply be a consequence of living in what Schell describes as an "upwardly mobile, design-conscious, divorce-prone" world, but it also tends to convey a basic lack of cultural confidence on the part of the daughters and thus a sense of their being thrown back into the families they have grown up in for explanations, validations, and identity reinforcement and definition.

Again, in the tradition of *The Woman Warrior*, *The Joy Luck Club* explores the subtle, perhaps never completely understood, influence of culture on those just beginning to live it. The mother-daughter tensions are both the articulation of the women's movement and the means of specifying the distinctness of Chinese and Chinese-American culture. As in *Woman Warrior*, behind the overt culture is an odd intuition of a ghost presence, at times a sense of madness waiting at the edge of existence. It is an unseen terror that runs through both the distinct social spectrum experienced by the mothers in China and the lack of such social definition in the daughters' lives. In this context the Joy Luck Club itself is the determination to hope in the face of constantly altering social situations and continually shifting rules.

The club is formed during the Japanese invasion of China, created by Jing-mei's mother as a deliberate defiance of the darkness of current events. With a mixture of desperation and frivolity, she and a group of friends meet, eat, laugh, tell stories, and play mah jong. She reasons, "we could hope to be lucky. That hope was our only joy." "It's not that we had no heart or eyes for pain. We were all afraid. We all had our miseries. But to despair was to wish back for something already lost. Or to prolong what was already unbearable."

It is the old China experience that manifests most definitely the enormous weight of fate in the lives of the characters. On the one hand, the constrictive burden is due to the position of women in that society. An-mei seems to regard the woman's role as an inescapable fate: "I was raised the Chinese way; I was taught to desire nothing, to swallow other people's misery, to eat my own bitterness. And even though I taught my daughter the opposite, still she came out the same way. . . . she was born a girl. And I was born to my mother and I was born a girl. All of us are like stairs, one step after another, going up and down, but all going the same way." Another mother, Lindo Jong, is the victim of a marriage arranged when she was only a child. In her struggle to extricate herself from the situation, she does not blame her family who made such arrangements but the society, the town where she grew up, a place she claims is frozen in custom at a time when the rest of China was beginning to change. Although the old culture places the family at its heart, as the experience of the women in this revolutionary situation demonstrates, its attitude toward women begins in the more fluid modern world to tear away at this fundamental unit, making the difficulty of mother-daughter bonding a crucial problem for the culture as a whole.

Ying-ying St. Clair blames herself more than her circumstances, but it is her early social circumstances that structure the experience that so haunts her and cripples her psychically. Situated higher in the social scale of old China than the other members of the club, she seems to fall as a child into a subconscious state from which she never fully recovers, a state that in the social context may stand as a paradigm for individual nightmare in a fragmenting culture. Hers is an episode with a fantasy/folk flavor and a motif of dreaming, which seems to represent a naive, open but mechanical relationship to culture—opposed to a vital reciprocity of being. Ying-ying (the childhood nickname here may be intended to suggest the regressive nature of her trauma) describes her adventures on a boat cruise during the Moon festival, which in her account becomes a symbolic episode, a psychological drifting from the fundamental reality of family. While everyone else sleeps, the little Ying-ying watches in fascination as some boys use a bird with a metal ring around its neck to catch fish. The bird serves its purpose, catching the fish but being unable to swallow them, its social function thus symbolically dependent on an intensely personal, intensely perverse individual frustration.

Finally the boys leave, but Ying-ying stays, "as if caught in a good dream" to watch "a sullen woman" clean fish and cut off the heads of chickens and turtles. As she begins to come back to self-consciousness, she notices that her fine party clothes are covered with the mess of these deaths— "spots of bloods, flecks of fish scales, bits of feather and mud." In the strangeness of her panic, she tries to cover the spots by painting her clothes with the turtle's blood. When her Amah appears, the servant is angry and strips off her clothes, using words that the child has never heard but from which she catches the sense of evil and, significantly, the threat of rejection by her mother. Left in her underwear, Ying-ying is alone at the boat's edge, suddenly looking at the moon, wanting to tell the Moon Lady her "secret wish." At this key moment in her young life, she falls into the water and is about to be drowned when miraculously she finds herself in a net with a heap of squirming fish. The fishing people who have saved her are of a class known to her, but a group from which she has previously been shielded. After some initial insensitive jokes about catching her, they attempt to restore her to her family group by hailing a floating pavilion to tell those aboard they have found the lost child. Instead of the family appearing to reclaim her, Ying-ying sees only strangers and a little girl who shouts, "That's not me. . . . I'm here. I didn't fall in the water."

What seems a bizarre, comically irrelevant mistake is the most revealing and shocking moment of the story, for it is as if her conscious self has suddenly appeared to deny her, to cast her permanently adrift in a life among strangers. To some degree this acute psychic sense of and fear of being abandoned by their family is a basic reality for all the mothers in this book, each of whose stories involve a fundamental separation from family, an ultimate wedge of circumstances between mother and child.

Though Ying-ying is finally restored to her family, the shock of separation has become too intense a reality. She tries to explain, "even though I was found—later that night after Amah, Baba, Uncle, and the others shouted for me along the waterway—I never believed my family found the same girl." Her self-accusations at the beginning of this story become a miniature autobiography: "For all these years I kept my mouth closed so selfish desires would not fall out. And because I remained quiet for so long now my daughter does not hear me. . . . I kept my true nature hidden. . . ." Later she accuses herself of becoming a ghost: "I willingly gave up my *chi*, the spirit that caused me so much pain." She fears that this abandonment of self has in some way been passed on to her daughter. "Now," she announces to herself, "I must tell my daughter everything. That she is the daughter of a ghost. She has no *chi*. This is my greatest shame. How can I leave this world without leaving her my spirit?" Her first narrative ends with her trapped in the legendary world of old China, still a child but with all the terrible insight into her later life: "I also remember what I asked the Moon Lady so long ago. I wished to be found."

The *chi* that she refers to may be impossible to render wholly into English, but it involves a fundamental self-respect, a desire to excel, a willingness to stand up for one's self and one's family, to demonstrate something to others. It may well be a quality that the daughters in the book lack, or that they possess in insufficient amounts. Veronica Wang states, "In the traditional Chinese society, women were expected to behave silently with submission but act heroically with strength. They were both sub-women and super-women." Possibly those cultural expectations, although almost totally erased in American culture, could still survive in residual roles when validated by a concept such as *chi*.

Whereas the major problem for the older generation had been the struggle against fate, the younger generation perceives their essential difficulty to involve the making of choices. The problem, as Rose Hsu Jordan defines it, is that America offers too many choices, "so much to think about, so much to decide. Each decision meant a turn in another direction." Like their mothers, many of the daughters are moving out or thinking of moving out, of family relationships, but such moves involve decisions about divorce, about whether their marriages are working out, about whether their husbands or future husbands fit into their lives.

One group of stories concerning the daughters features the struggle for maturity, a rather typical generational tension with the mothers. Perhaps surprisingly, the older women are for the most part not portrayed as pushing their daughters into an outmoded or inappropriate set of values and traditions, but they do insist on a basic cultural formulation. Lindo Jong's comments express a typical attitude: "I wanted my children to have the best combination: American circumstances and Chinese character." This sounds a note of compromise, but in reply to her daughter's declaration, "I'm my own person," she thinks, "How can she be her own person? When did I give her up?"

Curiously, in two instances, the generational tensions appear to have their origins in what seems a very American ambition. Waverly feels that her mother leeches off her chess achievements with an appropriating pride, and Jing-mei feels her mother, inspired by a competition with Waverly's mother as well as the belief that in America you could be anything you wanted, pushes her beyond her abilities, at least beyond her desires. The familiar cry

"You want me to be someone that I'm not!" accelerates to "I wish I wasn't your daughter. I wish you weren't my mother." and finally to "I wish I'd never been born! . . . I wish I were dead! Like them." The "them" are the other daughters her mother had been forced to abandon in China. This story of Jing-mei moves toward the kind of muted conclusion typical of most of the daughter stories: "unlike my mother, I did not believe I could be anything I wanted to be, I could only be me." There is the sense that this "me" lacks some vital centering, the cultural force that would provide its *chi*.

In the context of cultural analysis, the happiness of the conclusion seems only partially earned by what has preceded it. And the fact that the return and the reunion with the two half-sisters reflect almost exactly the author's own experience suggests that there may be more than a little biographical intrusion here. Ultimately, however, the book's final cultural argument seems to be that there is always a possibility for the isolated "me" to return home. At one time Jing-mei notes, "in a crowd of Caucasians, two Chinese people are already like family." As she makes the return trip to China in the last story, she feels she is at last becoming Chinese. What she discovers in her reunion with her Chinese half-sisters, in her father's story of her mother's separation from these children and from the mother's first husband, and in the photograph of her and her sisters is a renewed sense of her dead mother. The mother's living presence in them is the feeling Jing-mei has been searching for, the feeling of belonging in her family and of being at last in the larger family of China. In this case the feeling of cultural wholeness grows out of and seems dependent on a sense of family togetherness, but the return to the mainland certainly suggests a larger symbolic possibility, one, however, that must still cope with the actual barriers of geography, politics, and cultural distinctness.

In contrast to the treatments of generational differences in earlier books such as *Fifth Chinese Daughter*, both Maxine Hong Kingston and Amy Tan are empowered by current feminist ideas in their examinations of the Chinese-American woman's dilemma. In both *The Woman Warrior* and *The Joy Luck Club*, much of the focus springs out of the mother-daughter relationships and the way the diaspora has created a total contrast in the experiences of mother and daughter. Kingston's influential book tends to sort out the problems of a single "I" persona and is thus sharper in its dramatizations of the varied identity strands of a single individual, whereas Tan's multiplicity of first person narratives establishes a broader canvas with more feeling of fictional detachment between the reader and "I" and creates a voice for both generations. Both these authors testify to a rupture in the historical Chinese family unit as a result of the diaspora, but both seem to believe in a cultural healing. However, as her conclusion suggests, Tan seems to place more emphasis on the Chinese identity as the healing factor. Although perspectives are difficult to come by with contemporary work, the ability of both Kingston and Tan to render the experience of a culture through vividly dramatic individual narratives provides a sound basis for what seems to be a developing tradition of Chinese-American women's writing.

MARINA HEUNG

Daughter-Text/Mother-Text: Matrilineage in *Amy Tan's* Joy Luck Club

The critical literature on matrilineage in women's writings has already
achieved the status of a rich and evolving canon. At the same time, in
recognizing race, class, and gender as crucial determinants in writings by
women of color, some critics have indicated the need to develop a distinct
framework for understanding these works. For example, Dianne F. Sadoff
has examined the literature by African American women to note that "race
and class oppression intensify the black woman writer's need to discover an
untroubled matrilineal heritage." Referring to Alice Walker's adoption of
Zora Neale Hurston as a literary foremother, Sadoff shows how "in
celebrating her literary foremothers . . . the contemporary black woman
writer covers over more profoundly than does the white writer her
ambivalence about matrilineage, her own misreadings of precursors, and her
link to an oral as well as written tradition." Readers like Sadoff suggest that,
although matrilineage remains a consistent and powerful concern in the
female literary tradition, the recognition of culturally and historically specific
conditions in women's lives requires that we appropriately contextualize, and
thereby refine, our readings of individual texts.

In the realm of writings by Asian Americans, this work has begun.
Although it does not focus explicitly on the idea of matrilineage, Amy Ling's
Between Two Worlds: Women Writers of Chinese Ancestry is the first book to

From *Feminist Studies* Vol. 19, No. 3 (Fall 1993). © 1993 by Feminist Studies, Inc.

outline the literary tradition of one group of Asian American women. Her effort, Ling says, is inspired by Walker's "search for our mothers' gardens." Similarly, in a recent essay, Shirley Geok-lin Lim identifies Monica Sone's *Nisei Daughter* as a "mother text" for Joyce Kogawa's *Obasan*. In discussing these authors, Lim enumerates literary characteristics shared by Asian American and Asian Canadian women writers, such as "multiple presences, ambivalent stories, and circular and fluid narratives." Lim's analysis points toward a commonality between Sone and Kogawa and two other writers, Maxine Hong Kingston and Chuang Hua. In Kingston's *Woman Warrior* and Hua's *Crossings*, antirealistic narrative strategies and a provisional authorial stance correlate with experiences of cultural dislocation and of destabilized and fluid identities. Thus, the works of Sone, Kogawa, Kingston, and Hua collectively define an emerging canon cohering around concerns with racial, gender, and familial identity and the concomitant rejection of monolithic literary techniques.

In *Nisei Daughter, Obasan, The Woman Warrior*, and *Crossings*, the theme of matrilineage revolves around the figure of the daughter. With the exception of *Crossings* (which focuses on a daughter-father relationship), each of these works depicts how a daughter struggles toward self-definition by working through the mother-daughter dyad. The daughter's centrality thus places these writings firmly in the tradition delineated by Marianne Hirsch in *The Mother/Daughter Plot: Narrative, Psychoanalysis, Feminism*. Examining women's fiction from the eighteenth century through postmodernism, Hirsch notes the predominance of the daughter's voice and the silencing of the mother. This inscription of the "romance of the daughter" forms part of the feminist revision of the Freudian family plot.

> It is the woman as *daughter* who occupies the center of the global reconstruction of subjectivity and subject-object relation. The woman as *mother* remains in the position of other, and the emergence of feminine-daughterly subjectivity rests and depends on that continued and repressed process of *othering* the mother. . . . Daughter and mother are separated and forever trapped by the institution, the function of motherhood. They are forever kept apart by the text's daughterly perspective and signature: the mother is excluded from the discourse by the daughter who owns it.

Interestingly, Hirsch's few examples of departures from this pattern are drawn only from the writings of African American women. As she suggests, the scantiness of this sampling of "corrective" family romances, incorporating rather than repressing maternal discourse, reinforces the argument that feminist writers need to construct a new family romance to move the mother "from object to subject."

Published in 1989, Amy Tan's novel, *The Joy Luck Club*, is about four Chinese American daughters and their mothers. Like *The Woman Warrior* and *Crossings*, the novel contains autobiographical elements. In an interview, Tan describes how she was moved to establish a dialogue with her mother: "When I was writing, it was so much for my mother and myself . . . I wanted her to know what I thought about China and what I thought about growing up in this country. And I wanted those words to almost fall off the page so that she could just see the story, that the language would be simple enough, almost like a little curtain that would fall away." But despite Tan's explicit embrace of a daughter's perspective, *The Joy Luck Club* is remarkable for foregrounding the voices of mothers as well as of daughters. In the opening chapter of the novel, Jing-Mei Woo (also known as June) stands in for her recently deceased mother at an evening of mah-jong held by the Joy Luck Club, a group of elderly aunts and uncles. On this evening, three of her "Joy Luck aunties" give her money to fly to China to meet two half-sisters, twins who were abandoned by her mother during the war. In the last chapter of the novel, June makes this trip with her father. Her story (taking up four chapters) is told in her voice. The rest of the chapters are similarly narrated in the first person by three of June's coevals (Waverly Jong, Rose Jordan Hsu, and Lena St. Clair) and their mothers (Lindo Jong, An-Mei Hsu, and Ying-Ying St. Clair). Thus, totaling sixteen chapters in all, the novel interweaves seven voices, four of daughters, and three of mothers. In the way that it foregrounds maternal discourse, *The Joy Luck Club* materializes Marianne Hirsch's vision of a mother/daughter plot "written in the voice of mothers, as well as those of daughters . . . [and] in combining both voices [finds] a double voice that would yield a multiple female consciousness." But because the maternal voices in the novel bespeak differences derived from the mothers' unique positioning in culture and history, the subjectivities they inscribe, in counterpointing those of the daughters, also radically realign the mother/daughter plot itself.

In the chapter, "Double Face," in *The Joy Luck Club*, a scene implicitly illustrates the incompleteness of a model of the mother/daughter dyad defined only from the daughter's perspective. Here, the central motif is a mirror reflecting a mother and a daughter. Interweaving the themes of vision, recognition, and reflection, this scene shows the limits of viewing identification as an issue problematic for the daughter alone. The scene is set after Waverly has persuaded her mother to get her hair cut. Lindo is seated before a mirror as Waverly and Mr. Rory (the hairdresser) scrutinize her hairstyle. Sitting silently, Lindo listens to the two discuss her "as if [she] were not there." Her daughter translates Mr. Rory's questions for her, even though Lindo can understand English perfectly well. When Waverly speaks directly to her, she does so loudly, "as if [Lindo has] lost [her] hearing." But because this scene is narrated from Lindo's perspective, her vision and subjectivity are in fact in control. Even as her daughter seems determined to nullify her presence, Lindo sees the superficial social ease between Waverly and Mr. Rory as typical of how "Americans don't really look at one another when talking." Despite her silence and apparent acquiescence, she interposes herself nonverbally through her smiles and her alternation between her "Chinese face" and her "American face" ("the face Americans think is Chinese, the one they cannot understand").

The scene turns on Mr. Rory's sudden exclamation at seeing the uncanny resemblance between mother and daughter reflected in the mirror. Lindo notes Waverly's discomfiture: "'The same cheeks.' [Waverly] says. She points to mine and then pokes her cheeks. She sucks them outside in to look like a starved person." Waverly's response exhibits her "matrophobia," defined by Adrienne Rich as the daughter's fear of "becoming one's mother." Feminists have analyzed the daughter's ambivalence toward identification with the mother, but Lindo's response in this scene allows us to consider identification from a maternal perspective. Much as Lindo possesses a "double face," she also has access to a "double vision." Seeing herself mirrored in her daughter, she recalls her own mother in China.

> And now I have to fight back my feelings. These two faces, I think, so much the same! The same happiness, the same sadness, the same good fortune, the same faults.
> I am seeing myself and my mother, back in China, when I was a young girl.

With her "double vision," Lindo is not threatened by her daughter's attempted erasure of her; in fact, she is moved by her daughter's resemblance to her, even as she registers Waverly's response. Lindo's perspective is informed by her personal history and by her ability to bridge time and cultures. At the same time, Lindo's knowledge of family history provides one key to her sense of ethnic identity. As critics have noted, in writings by Asian American women, issues of matrilineage are closely bound with those of acculturation and race. Thus, Shirley Lim writes: "The essential thematics of maternality is also the story of race . . . [The mother] is the figure not only of maternality but also of racial consciousness." But in presenting the mother as the potent symbol of ethnic identity, Lim implicitly adopts the perspective of the daughter. In her scheme, the mother's primary role is to set into motion the daughter's working through toward a separate selfhood and a new racial identity. Yet this elevation of the daughter as the figure around whom the "dangers of rupture and displaced selves" converge marginalizes maternal subjectivity and voicing. But surely the issues of identification, differentiation, and ethnic identity have meaning for mothers as well, and this meaning must to a significant degree devolve from their relationships with their own mothers. As exemplified in this episode in "Double Face," *The Joy Luck Club* moves maternality to the center. It locates subjectivity in the maternal and uses it as a pivot between the past and the present. In so doing, it reclaims maternal difference and reframes our understanding of daughterly difference as well.

Recent feminist revisions of the Freudian Oedipal family romance assume a culturally and historically specific model of the nuclear family. In her influential book, *The Reproduction of Mothering: Psychoanalysis and the Sociology of Gender*, Nancy Chodorow shows how the institution of motherhood based on childcare provided by women sustains the central problematics of separation and differentiation for daughters. Using a paradigm that is white, middle-class, and Western, Chodorow's analysis is not universally applicable. In this vein, Dianne F Sadoff and Ruth Perry and Martine Watson Brownley show how the Black family, distorted through the history of slavery in particular, needs to be understood through alternative models. Such a culturally specific critique needs to be applied to the traditional Chinese family as well. Because of their historical devaluation, women in the Chinese family are regarded as disposable property or detachable appendages despite their crucial role in maintaining the family line through childbearing. Regarded as expendable "objects to be invested in or bartered," the marginal status of Chinese women shows itself in their forced transfer from natal families to other families through the practice of arranged marriage, concubinage, adoption, and pawning. The position of women—as daughters, wives, and mothers—in Chinese society is therefore markedly provisional, with their status and expendability fluctuating according to their families' economic circumstances, their ability to bear male heirs, and the proclivities of authority figures in their lives.

This pattern of radical rupture within families is illustrated by the family histories of An-Mei, Lindo, and Ying-Ying in *The Joy Luck Club*. As a child, An-Mei is raised by her grandmother; she has only confused memories of her mother. One day, when her grandmother is dying, her mother appears and removes her to Shanghai; An-Mei is then adopted into a new family where her mother is the fourth concubine of a wealthy merchant.

In contrast to An-Mei, Lindo is removed from her natal family through marriage, not adoption. At age two, Lindo is engaged to a young boy who is a stranger to her. A bride in an arranged marriage at sixteen, Lindo finally succeeds in freeing herself through a ruse by which she convinces her husband's family to find a concubine for him.

Like Lindo, Ying-Ying is chosen as a bride by a stranger, a man who associates deflowering her with the act of *kai gwa* ("open the watermelon"). A "wild and stubborn" girl in her youth, Ying-Ying's spirit is destroyed in this brutal marriage. Later, when she is pregnant, her husband leaves her for another woman; she decides to get an abortion.

In *The Joy Luck Club*, family allegiances are complicated and disrupted within a kinship system in which blood ties are replaced by a network of alternate affiliations. When Lindo is engaged to the son of the Huang family, for instance, her family relationships are immediately reconfigurated. Her mother starts treating her "as if [she] belonged to someone else," and she begins to be referred to as her future mother-in-law's daughter.

For An-Mei, the breakage and realignment of relationships involving parents and siblings are even more radical and arbitrary. When her mother removes her from her grandmother's household, her brother—her mother's first son—is left behind because patrilineal claims on male children cannot be challenged. After her adoption into her new family, An-Mei is introduced to three other wives in the family—each a potential surrogate mother. For instance, her mother tells her to call the Second Wife "Big Mother." She also acquires a new brother, Syaudi, who now becomes her "littlest brother." But An-Mei has to undergo one final upheaval when she finds out that Syaudi is truly her brother by blood and not adoption. This happens when her mother's attendant tells her how An-Mei's mother was forced into concubinage and bore a son; this son was then adopted by the Second Wife as her own. In this way, An-Mei makes a shocking discovery: "That was how I learned that the baby Syaudi was really my mother's son, my littlest brother."

Unlike Lindo and An-Mei, Suyuan Woo (June's mother) sees her family dispersed as a result of cataclysmic historical events. During the Japanese bombardment of Kweilin during the war, she is forced to flee south without her husband; discarding her possessions along the way and desperate for food, she finally abandons her twin daughters on the road. Later in America, her new daughter, June, grows up with the knowledge of a truncated family, haunted by her mother's words: "Your father is not my first husband. You are not those babies."

These stories of disrupted family connections, of divided, multiplied, and constantly realigned perceptions of kinship, constitute a pattern clearly diverging from the monolithic paradigm of the nuclear family. In *The Joy Luck Club*, their experiences of broken and fluctuating family bonds inspire Lindo, An-Mei, and Ying-Ying to construct stories of bonding with the mother precisely in answer to their memories of profound rupture and abandonment. Speaking from their experiences of mother loss, these immigrant mothers offer altered versions of the "romance of the daughter." Whereas typical versions of this romance highlight generational conflict and the repression of the mother, An-Mei, Lindo, and Ying-Ying construct consoling tales enacting a fantasy of symbiosis with the maternal. Recalling her first sight of her mother after a long separation, An-Mei describes how their exchange of gazes locks them into instant identification: "[My mother] looked up. And when she did, I saw my own face looking back at me." An-Mei also privileges her mother's story about two turtles joined through suffering; from this parable of shared grief, An-Mei derives a message connecting her to her mother: "That was our fate, to live like two turtles seeing the watery world together from the bottom of the little pond." In this way, An-Mei transforms common experiences of pain and victimization into testimonials of mother/daughter bonding. Similarly, instead of feeling outrage at her mother's collaboration in her arranged betrothal and marriage, Lindo actually chooses collusion with her mother, behaving as the proper daughter-in-law so that her mother will not lose face.

However, years later, in America, Lindo's assertion of instinctive bonding with her mother is contested by new realities. She comes to regret how her mother "did not see how [her] face changed over the years. How [her] mouth began to droop. How [she] began to worry but still did not lose [her] hair. . . ." Acknowledging these inevitable changes in herself, Lindo implicitly admits the loss of symbiosis. Her transplantation into American culture and her advancing age have made her face no longer a perfect match of her mother's. Quite simply, her new "double face" reflects her changed cultural identity: "I think about our two faces. I think about my intentions. Which one is American? Which one is Chinese? Which one is better? If you show one, you must also sacrifice the other."

At the same time, Lindo's recognition of her own doubled identity has implications for how she understands her relationship with her daughter. Like her, Waverly is the product of two cultures, but Lindo sees that Waverly's experience of cultural mixing is different from her own: "Only her skin and hair are Chinese. Inside—she is all American-made." The otherness of her daughter's hybridized self for Lindo makes it unlikely that mother and daughter can achieve perfect identification: the burden of differences in personal history and cultural conditioning is too great. Yet, in *The Joy Luck Club*, the mothers' ability to accept their own loss of the maternal image also enables them to separate from their daughters. As Ying-Ying says: "I think this to myself even though I love my daughter. She and I have shared the same body. There is part of her mind that is part of mine. But when she was born, she sprang from me like a slippery fish, and has been swimming away from me since." Thus, in Tan's novel, the maternal experience of generational conflict and differentiation takes into account the realities of cultural difference; through this awareness, the Joy Luck mothers can negotiate their ambivalences about their daughters' desires for cultural assimilation and autonomous selfhood.

As the essential medium of subjectivity, language is the ground for playing out cultural differences. Gloria Anzaldúa has written about her language use as an insignia of her "borderlands" identity situated between Mexico and America: "Ethnic identity is twin skin to linguistic identity—I am my language. Until I can accept as legitimate Chicano Texas Spanish, Tex Mex and all the other languages I speak, I cannot accept the legitimacy of myself." The speaker of this "language of Borderlands," Anzaldúa suggests, has the freedom to "switch codes" at will; it is a "bastard" language located at the "juncture of culture [where] languages cross-pollinate and are revitalized." In *The Joy Luck Club*, the language of the mothers—their border language— marks their positioning between two cultures. However, in exposing linguistic limits, the novel also argues for reclaiming language as an instrument of intersubjectivity and dialogue, and as a medium of transmission from mothers to daughters.

In the novel, the daughters understand Chinese, but they speak English exclusively. The mothers, in contrast, speak a version of Anzaldúa's "language of the Borderlands," a *patois* of Chinese and English that often confuses their daughters. Observing her aunties, June thinks: "The Joy Luck aunties begin to make small talk, not really listening to each other. They speak in their special language, half in broken English, half in their own Chinese dialect." Embarrassing at times to the daughters, this language is a form of self-inscription in an alien culture, a way of preserving significance in the new reality of America. For one, the nuggets of foreign words incorporated into this speech duplicate aspects of self-identity that have no equivalent in another language. Words like *lihai*, *chuming*, and *nengkan* must remain in their original Chinese in order to retain their power and meaning. For Ying-Ying, the essence of her youthful character before she became a lost soul, a "ghost," is contained in the word *lihai*: "When I was a young girl in Wushi, I was *lihai*. Wild and stubborn. I wore a smirk on my face. Too good to listen." Her confidence in her special knowledge is expressed by *chuming*, referring to her "inside knowledge of things." For Rose, *nengkan* expresses her mother's ability to act on pure will and determination, as shown in An-Mei's summoning of her son's spirit after he has drowned at the beach. On another occasion, An-Mei's command of this hybrid language enables her to articulate, on her daughter's behalf, Rose's disorientation during her divorce. When An-Mei complains that Rose's psychiatrist is making her *hulihudu* and *heimongmong*, Rose ponders: "It was true. And everything around me seemed to be *heimongmong*. These were words I have never thought about in English terms. I suppose the closest in meaning would be 'confused' and 'dark fog'."

In discussing the use of "multilanguedness" in women's writings, Patricia Yaeger suggests that the "incorporation of a second language can function . . . as a subversive gesture representing an alternative form of speech which can both disrupt the repressions of authoritative discourse and still welcome or shelter themes that have not yet found a voice in the . . . primary language." Although Yaeger is concerned with specific narrative strategies used in women's texts, her analysis has resonance for the significance of maternal speech in *The Joy Luck Club*. Without being overtly political or subversive, the mothers' bilingualism in the novel is nonetheless strategic. Switching from English to Chinese can express rejection and anger, as when June's mother berates her for not trying hard enough at her piano playing: "'So ungrateful,' I heard her mutter in Chinese. 'If she had as much talent as she has temper, she would be famous now.'" Or, the switching of codes may initiate a shift into a different register of intimacy, as when the same mother speaks in Chinese when making her daughter a gift of a jade pendant. To express her resentment against an American husband who persistently puts English words in her mouth, Ying-Ying uses Chinese exclusively with her daughter. Deliberate deformations of language, too, are used to convey veiled criticisms, as when Ying-Ying snidely refers to her daughter's profession as an architect as "arty-tecky," and An-Mei dismisses Rose's psychiatrist as "psyche-tricks." Finally, the use of Chinese is a form of resistance to a hegemonic culture. In the following exchange, initiated when Waverly slyly asks about the difference between Jewish and Chinese mahjong, Lindo's use of Chinese is self-reflexive; her switch from English to Chinese in itself expresses her sense of cultural difference and superiority.

> "Entirely different kind of playing," she said in her English explanation voice. "Jewish mah jong, they watch only for their own tile, play only with their eyes."
>
> Then she switched to Chinese: "Chinese mah jong, you must play using your head, very tricky. You must watch what everybody else throws away and keep that in your head as well. And if nobody plays well, then the game becomes like Jewish mah jong. Why play? There's no strategy. You're just watching people make mistakes."

In *The Joy Luck Club*, "multilanguedness" bears the imprint of their speakers' unique cultural positioning, but this assertion of difference is also vexed by its potential to confuse and exclude. For the daughters, the special meaning of maternal language requires translation. After her mother's death, June thinks: "My mother and I never really understood each other. We translated each other's meanings and I seemed to hear less than what was said, while my mother heard more." Another question is how effectively maternal language functions as a medium of transmission between generations. The mothers in the novel worry that the family history and knowledge preserved in their hybrid language will be elided after their deaths. At one point, June comes to understand how important it is for her aunties to preserve the meaning of "joy luck": "They see that joy and luck do not mean the same to their daughters, that to these closed American-born minds 'joy luck' is not a word, it does not exist. They see daughters who will bear grandchildren born without any connecting hope from generation to generation."

Hybrid in its origins, maternal language in *The Joy Luck Club* possesses multiple, even contradictory, meanings. As an assertion of cultural identity, it both communicates and obfuscates. At the same time, it stands in counterpoint to maternal silence. To the daughters, maternal silence hints at "unspeakable tragedies," and the maternal injunction to "bite back your tongue" binds daughters and mothers in a cycle of self-perpetuating denial. Yet both daughters and mothers resist this bind. The Joy Luck aunties, after all, plead frantically with June to tell her mother's—and, by implication, their own—history ("Tell them, tell them"). Similarly, Lena is aware of the power of the unspoken: "I always thought it mattered, to know what is the worst possible thing that can happen to you, to know how you can avoid it, to not be drawn by the magic of the unspeakable." Finally, it is the incomprehension enforced by silence that keeps mothers "othered" in the eyes of their daughters. An-Mei, for instance, is dismissed by Suyuan as a woman with "no spine" who "never thought about what she was doing," and Ying-Ying is seen by June as the "weird aunt, someone lost in her own world." As for Lindo, her special insight allows her to understand why her daughter and her friends see her as a "backward Chinese woman."

In the tradition of breaking silence that has become one of the shaping myths in the writings of women of color, maternal silence in the novel is transformed from a medium of self-inscription and subjectivity into an instrument of intersubjectivity and dialogue. For the mothers, storytelling heals past experiences of loss and separation; it is also a medium for rewriting stories of oppression and victimization into parables of self-affirmation and individual empowerment. For the Joy Luck mothers, the construction of a self in identification with a maternal figure thus parallels, finally, a revisioning of the self through a reinterpretation of the past:

In Lindo's case, the brutality of a forced marriage is transformed, through its retelling, into a celebration of courage and resistance. She recalls looking into a mirror on the day of her wedding and being surprised at seeing her own purity and strength: "Underneath the scarf I still knew who I was. I made a promise to myself: I would always remember my parents' wishes, but I would never forget myself." Through a clever scheme, Lindo escapes from her marriage. After arriving in America, she chooses her second husband, getting him to propose by inserting a message inside a fortune cookie. Because all her jewelry was taken from her during her first marriage, she makes sure that she receives genuine gold jewelry from her husband and as gifts that she buys for herself: "And every few years, when I have a little extra money, I buy another bracelet. I know what I'm worth. They're always twenty-four carats, all genuine."

For An-Mei and Ying-Ying, self-articulation remedies early teachings in silence and self-denial. Both begin to recall painful memories when they see how their speech can save their daughters. Ying-Ying is stirred to speak directly to Lena when she sees her daughter's unhappy marriage. At one time a "tiger girl" who gave up her *chi* ("breath" or "lifeforce") in an unhappy marriage, Ying-Ying now recognizes that her daughter has "become like a ghost, disappear." The emptiness of Lena's life—with her fancy swimming pool, her Sony Walkman, and cordless phone—is apparent to her. Watching Rose go through a difficult divorce, An-Mei recalls her own mother's dying words, that "she would rather kill her own weak spirit so she could give me a stronger one." In the end, An-Mei and Ying-Ying find their voices: Ying-Ying to "wake up" Rose and Lena to "penetrate her skin and pull her to where she can be saved."

The stories of their lives are the mothers' gifts to their daughter in the spirit with which the Joy Luck Club was originally founded. Years ago, June's mother formed the club in Kweilin in order to transmute the painful history of women like herself into a communal expression of defiance and hope, so that "each week [they] could forget past wrongs done to us . . . hope to be lucky." In breaking silence, these mothers reproduce the past as tales of "joy" and "luck." Like the scar on An-Mei's neck that her mother rubs in order to bring back a painful memory, these narrations effect a passage from pain to catharsis, moving their tellers from inward knowledge to intersubjective dialogue. Significantly, each of the mother's stories suspends its mode of address between "I" and "you." Thus, the closing sentence in Lindo's story is: "I will ask my daughter what she thinks." In inviting the daughters' interjections, the shift from interior monologue to dialogue enables the mothers to discover how they will mediate between the past and the present for their daughters. Their choices take them on the path, described by Kim

Chernin, by which mothers can become "co-conspirator[s]" with their daughters to stand "outside the oppressive system, united in some common effort." Chernin suggests that a mother must ally herself with her daughter's struggle by first acknowledging that she too has passed "knowingly through a similar time of urgency and [has] been able to develop beyond it." She concludes that a mother's entry into collaboration with her daughter involves a commitment to speech. She must be willing to "admit her conflict and ambivalence, acknowledge the nearness or actuality of breakdown, become fully conscious of her discontent, the hushed, unspoken sense of her life's failure." After all, as Adrienne Rich proposes, "the quality of the mother's life—however embattled and unprotected—is her primary bequest to her daughter." Thus, the determination to provide models of "courageous mothering," as envisioned by Rich is finally the subtext of the stories told by stories in *The Joy Luck Club*. Not the least of this maternal courage is the mothers' reclaiming of storytelling as an act of self-creation, one by which they enact, with a full complement of ambivalence and doubt, their passage from loss and dispossession to hope and affirmation.

In the opening story of the novel, June represents her recently deceased mother at a meeting of the Joy Luck Club. Feeling out of place, she imagines that the three Joy Luck aunties "must wonder now how someone like me can take my mother's place." The three aunties give her $1,200 to travel to China to meet her twin half-sisters, saying, "You must see your sisters and tell them about your mother's death. . . . But most important, you must tell them about her life." But until the moment of the meeting, June asks herself: "How can I describe to them in Chinese about our mother's life?"

The four stories told from June's point of view constitute pure family romance, in which family members are separated, lost, and reunited. The guiding spirit of this myth is June's mother, Suyuan. However, as told by June, the story is unmistakably the daughter's version of the family romance, in which a mother's death opens up the space for a daughter's recuperation of a lost maternal image. Even while protesting that she doesn't know enough to tell her mother's story, June nevertheless proves correct her aunties' insistence: "Your mother is in your bones! . . . her mind . . . has become your mind." She starts cooking the same dishes for her father as her mother did; one evening she finds herself standing at the kitchen window, in imitation of her mother, rapping at a neighborhood cat. Arriving in Shenzhen, China, just over the border from Hong Kong, she starts to feel different: "I can feel the skin on my forehead tingling, my blood rushing through a new course, my bones aching with a familiar old pain. And I think,

My mother was right. I am becoming Chinese." Earlier she imagines that by dying her mother has left her, "gone back to China to get these babies." But as it turns out, it is she who is returning to China as her mother's emissary. Arriving in China with her father, she hears the final episode of her mother's story: how her mother was forced to abandon her twin babies and continued her search for them through the years. Turning to her father for this history, June urges him to tell it in Chinese: "No, tell me in Chinese. . . . Really, I can understand."

During the scene of June's reunion with her sisters, the rebounding of mirror images enacts a climactic moment, binding mother to daughter and sister to sister.

> Somebody shouts, "She's arrived!" And then I see her. Her short hair. Her small body. And that same look on her face. She has the back of her hand pressed hard against her mouth. She is crying as though she had gone through a terrible ordeal and were happy it is over.
>
> And I know it's not my mother, yet it is the same look she had when I was five and had disappeared all afternoon, for such a long time, that she was convinced that I was dead. And when I miraculously appeared, sleepy-eyed, crawling from underneath my bed, she wept and laughed, biting the back of her hand to make sure it was true.
>
> And now I see her again, two of her, waving, and in one hand is a photo, the Polaroid I sent them. As soon as I get beyond the gate, we run toward each other, all three of us embracing, all hesitations and expectations gone.

In this encounter, sisterly and maternal identities are blurred, and through the recovery of lost sisters, the foundling myth is conflated with the romance of the daughter. Looking into her sisters' faces, June also sees mirrored in them part of her own ethnic identity: "And now I also see what part of me is Chinese. It is so obvious. It is my family. It is in our blood. After all these years, it can finally be let go."

At the beginning of the novel, while representing her mother at the Joy Luck Club, June muses: "And I am sitting at my mother's place at the mah jong table, on the East, where things begin." June's story ends with her further east still in China, where there is yet another beginning. The meeting of the three sisters makes their generation whole again; resembling their mother as well as each other, the sisters' mutual identification recuperates maternal loss. Now June remembers her mother's remark to her: "Our whole family is gone. It is just you and I." With June's reunion with her sisters, however, the continuity of the family—but through the female line of descent—is reestablished. And finally, since the word the sisters speak upon recognizing each other—"Mama, Mama"—has common currency across cultures, matrilineage here signifies not only the possibility of a nurturing sisterhood but also the melding of crosscultural linkages.

Although June's story matches the pattern of the idealized family romance, the overall structure of the novel offers such closure as a provisional possibility only. As we have seen, although maternal speech in the novel turns in the direction of intersubjectivity, this movement is tentative and incomplete. The narratives by Lindo, An-Mei, and Waverly shift from "I" to "you," but the absence of a reciprocal progression in their daughters' stories (from a daughterly "I" to the maternal "you") suggests the truncation of a truly dialogic process. Further, the novel's overall structure consciously resists any attempt to shape it definitively. As Valerie Miner has noted, the novel is "narrated horizontally as well as vertically." Thus, June's symbolically complete and symmetrical story is contained within an overarching framework wrapping around a grouping of other stories whose arrangement is neither causal nor linear. Thus, although June's story offers closure in its progression from loss to recuperation, the other narratives are grouped in loose juxtaposition with each other. The mothers' stories are included in the first and last of the four main units in the novel and recount incidents in China; the daughters' stories appear in the middle two sections and are set in the immediate past or proximate present.

On closer reading, even the autonomy of each story as a clear-cut unit begins to dissolve, giving way to a subterranean pattern of resonances and motifs erasing the definite boundaries between individual narratives. Under this scrutiny, actions and motifs mirror each other from story to story, undermining absolute distinctions of character and voice. Thus, the formative moment of Lindo's story, when she looks into the mirror on her wedding day and pledges "never to forget" herself, is duplicated by June's standing in front of a mirror as a teenager, contemplating her self-worth under the assault of her mother's expectations: "The girl staring back at me was angry, powerful. This girl and I were the same. I had new thoughts, willful thoughts, or rather thoughts filled with lots of won'ts. I won't let her change me, I promised myself. I won't be what I'm not.'" Similarly, Ying-Ying learns from the Moon Lady that the woman is "yin [from] the darkness within" and the man is "yang, bright with lighting our minds." Ying-Ying's lesson about the yin and the yang is echoed in Rose's description of her marriage: "We became inseparable, two halves creating the whole: yin and yang. I was victim to his hero. I was always in danger and he was always rescuing me." Or, to cite a final example of how the novel converges particular motifs: just before Rose's divorce, An-Mei tells her daughter that her husband is probably "doing monkey business with someone else"; Rose scoffs at her mother's intuition, but a later discovery proves her mother right. Elsewhere, Lena similarly remarks on her own mother's "mysterious ability to see things before they happen"; in her case, Ying-Ying's uncanny foresight, like An-Mei's, predicts the collapse of Lena's marriage.

Signaling the author's intent to undermine the independence of individual narrative units, even the chapter titles, by connecting motifs between disparate stories, seem interchangeable. The title of Rose's story, "Half and Half," is echoed at the end of a story narrated by June when, turning to the piano she has abandoned for many years, she plays two old tunes and realizes that they are "two halves of the same song." The theme of "half and half" is continued in the story told by Waverly, in which her mother tells her that she has inherited half of her character traits from each parent: "half of everything inside you is from me, your mother's side, from the Sun clan in Taiyuan." In another illustration of how thematic echoes proliferate in the novel, this same story, entitled "Four Directions," encourages us to trace its various motifs elsewhere. Waverly's "good stuff" that she has inherited from her mother reiterates the theme of "best quality" that is continued in another story told by June: in "Best Quality," June's mother chides her for not wanting the best for herself. Meanwhile, the theme of "Four Directions" takes us back to the first story in the novel, where we find June and her aunties seated at the mah-jong table, each occupying one of its four directions.

Obviously, the notion of "four directions" is emblematic of the novel's centrifugal structure. At one point, Lena asks: "How can the world in all its chaos come up with so many coincidences, so many similarities and exact opposites?" Or, as June intones, in a more complaining mood, "It's the same old thing, everyone talking in circles." With its mirrored motifs and interchangeable characterizations, *The Joy Luck Club* demands a reading that is simultaneously diachronic and synchronic. Aligning itself with the modernist tradition of spatial form in narrative, the novel defeats any effort to read it according to linear chronology alone. Instead, the reader's construction of interconnections between motif, character, and incident finally dissolves individualized character and plot and instead collectivizes them into an aggregate meaning existing outside the individual stories themselves.

The multivalent structure of *The Joy Luck Club* resists reduction to simple geometric designs; nevertheless, two figures—the rectangle and the circle—help to chart Tan's play on the theme of maternality. As the novel begins, June takes her place with three Joy Luck aunties around the mah-jong table. Her position at one of the table's cardinal points determines the direction of her journey east which ends in China. At the end point of June's story, the trope of the rectangle merges with that of the circle: June's arrival in China brings her full circle to the place where her mother's story began, and her meeting with her half-sisters sets into motion a circulation of mirrored relationships blurring identities, generations, and languages. Because it repudiates linearity and symmetry, the circle is a privileged motif in feminist writings, one that suggests the possibility of reconfiguring traditional familial dynamics and dismantling the hierarchical arrangements of the Oedipal triangle and the patriarchal family. For instance, in her book on the reclamation of the pre-Oedipal in women's novels, Jean Wyatt envisions "the possibility . . . of imagining alternative family relations based on preoedipal patterns—family circles whose fluidity of interchange challenges the rigid gender and generational hierarchies of the patriarchal family." In Wyatt's analysis, there persists, in women's writings, the fantasy of a nurturant family where "family members come forward to share the work of fostering others' development [so that] the responsibility for nurturing [is extended] to a whole circle of 'mothering' people."

In *The Joy Luck Club*, the discrete identities of familial members are woven into a collectivized interchangeability through the novel's parataxis—its use of contiguous juxtapositions of voices, narratives, and motifs. Through the novel's interweaving of time frames and voices, three generations of women are included within a relational network linking grandmothers, mothers, daughters, aunts, and sisters. For these women, however, mutual nurturance does not arise from biological or generational connections alone; rather, it is an act affirming consciously chosen allegiances. As Wyatt suggests, mothering as a "reciprocal activity" generally presupposes "a strong mother figure who has a central position in the family," but even "when the mother is not there, the circle remains, its diffuse bonds extends to a circle of equals who take turns nurturing each other." In *The Joy Luck Club*, the death of June's mother, Suyuan, invites the Joy Luck aunties to step into the circle of "mothering reciprocity"; indeed, it is Suyuan's absence that inaugurates the meeting between June and her half-sisters, when they confirm their mutual identification as each other's sisters *and* mothers.

As we have seen, the maternal voices in *The Joy Luck Club* begin to shift from "I" to "you" to engage the discrete subjectivities of mother and daughter in a tentative exchange of recognitions and identifications. In the same way, the novel's resonant structure and its use of parataxis effectively write the reader into the text as a crucial participant in the making of meaning. The reader of *The Joy Luck Club* is a weaver of intricate interconnections who must, like Suyuan's unraveling of an old sweater, randomly "pull out a kinky thread of yarn, anchoring it to a piece of cardboard, [roll] with a sweeping rhythm, [and] start [a] story." This way of engaging the reader as an active constructor of meaning allows the feminist novel to project a community of sisterly readers. In tracing a family history that blurs the demarcations between the roles of mothers, daughters, and sisters, *The Joy Luck Club* breaks down the boundary between text and reader in order to proffer the notions of sisterhood as a literary construction and as a community constituted through the act of reading. At once disintegrative and constructive in its operations, the novel holds its dual impulses in unresolved suspension and fulfills its fundamentally transformative project— a mutation from daughter-text to mother-text to sister-text.

BEN XU

Memory and the Ethnic Self:
Reading Amy Tan's The Joy Luck Club

The Chinese-American milieu in a San Francisco neighborhood furnishes the main contingent of characters in Amy Tan's *The Joy Luck Club*. What the four families in that book, the Woos, Jongs, Hsus, and St. Clairs, have in common is mother-daughter relations. The mothers are all first generation immigrants from mainland China, speaking very little English and remaining cultural aliens in their new world. The daughters are all born and educated in America, some even married to "foreigners." Within the microcultural structure of family, the only means available for mothers to ensure ethnic continuity is to recollect the past and to tell tales of what is remembered. Lamenting the failing marriage of Lena, her daughter, and Lena's unfamiliarity with the "Chinese ways of thinking," Ying-ying St. Clair voices the anxiety and helplessness shared by all the mothers in the book:

> All her life, I have watched her as though from another shore. And now I must tell her everything about my past. It is the only way to penetrate her skin and pull her to where she can be saved.

In her mother's eyes, because Lena, without a memory of the past, allows herself to be borne by the bustle of life, she doesn't know who she is, and

From *MELUS* Vol. 19, No. 1 (Spring 1994). © 1994 by the Society for the Study of Multi-Ethnic Literature of the U.S.

cannot hold herself together. It may be true that through her mother's memory, Lena will learn to share a belief in certain rules, roles, behaviors and values which provide, within the family and the overseas Chinese community, a functional ethos and a medium of communication. But will she, even if she unexpectedly finds herself confronted by an hour which has a special connection with her mother's past, have access to her mother's deeply buried anxiety, psychic need, specific mental habits, and life-world perception? Can she really share her mother's unrepeatable life-experience? Can she ever learn how to overstep her own existential limits through her mother's story? What if she has to take cognizance of a barrier in her present existence that will eternally be a barrier between her and her mother? These questions can be asked not only about Lena, but also about all the other daughters in *The Joy Luck Club*. I will take a close look here at the conflict between the two generations of the book and the existential unrepeatability that separates them. Through examining the complexity of the operations of memory, I will also explore how the recollection and narration of the past are related to a present sense of ethnic identity.

"Memory" is an intellectually seductive concept, capable of drawing on diverse literatures, from the cognitive concerns of speculative philosophy to experimental psychological probes of the processing-storage-retrieval function of mind. Yet because the intellectual roots are so diffuse, and the connotations quite varied, I should clarify the two basic assumptions that I make when I use this term in my discussion of ethnic identity in *The Joy Luck Club*: first, a premise of the narrative construction of memory, and second, an emphasis on its social-psychological mechanism.

Most of the philosophical thinking on memory lapses almost inadvertently into the idiom of the static picture by conceiving of memory as a particular content of the mind, as an "image," a "presentation," an "impression," and so on. However, it is not just that we have "images," "pictures," and "views" of ourselves in memory, but that we also have "stories" and "narratives" to tell about the past which both shape and convey our sense of self. Our sense of what has happened to us is entailed not in actual happenings but in meaningful happenings, and the meanings of our past experience, as I will explore and defend in my reading of *The Joy Luck Club*, are constructs produced in much the same way that narrative is produced. Identity, as well as the implicated self-definition and self-narrative, almost certainly will be activated from memory. Recent social-psychological studies have shown that self-images bring forth a host of intricately related self-knowledge and self-identity, whose information, values, and related beliefs are socially situated as well as psychologically useful. Such understanding of the social-psychological mechanism of memory narrative is also implied in recent studies of narrative. Hayden White suggests that, in the narrative of individual life as well as in the narrative of history, the meaning of a given set of events, which he recognizes as taking the form of recurring tropical enfigurations, is not the same as the story they consist of. Using, as a guideline, his differentiation of two kinds of narrative meanings without committing to his tropological explanation of them, we may, in memory narrative, distinguish its life-story from the existential perception it entails. If the life-story is marked by a seeming actuality, the existential perception is what transforms the casual daily events into a functioning mentality or an existential concern that is not self-evident.

This bifurcate view of memory narrative permits us to consider a specific life-story as imagery of existential themes or problems about which the story is told, and the existential perception as a comprehensive context in which meaningful questions can be asked about the factual events of that life-story (what, how, and especially why). A functioning mentality, such as the survival mentality which characterizes all the mother characters in *The Joy Luck Club*, hardly enters into view with factual occurrences. It manifests itself only in the distribution of existential themes of the memory narrative. Memory narrative does not represent a perfect equivalent of the events it purports to describe. It goes beyond the actuality of events to the determination of their coherency as an existential situation, and this general picture of life in turn assigns exemplary values to the events which are awakened in memory by a functioning mentality.

This awakening of memory by a person's present mentality is ilustrated by Ying-ying St. Clair's story of her childhood. When Ying-ying was four years old, she got separated from her parents on a Moon Festival trip to a scenic lake, and while watching a performance of Moon Lady, she made a wish which she could not remember for many decades. It is only after her first broken marriage, and a second one to a kind but alien Irishman, and many "years washing away the pain, the same way carvings on stone are worn down by water," when she was "moving every year closer to the end of my life," that she remembers that, on that night, as a child of four, she "wished to be found."

Of the four mother characters in *The Joy Luck Club*, Ying-ying had the happiest childhood. Her family was very wealthy and took good care of her. Her getting lost from her family on a festival trip was no more than a small accident with no harmful consequences. However, this insignificant incident in her early childhood is remembered as an emblem of her unfortunate life. This is the memory of a survivor of bad times, who has lost her capacity to remember a different life even though she did once experience it. The memory itself has become a psychic defense, which helps to justify her social disengagement, her fatalistic perception of the world as a system of total control, and her fascination with extreme situations and with the possibility of applying their lessons to everyday life.

Ying-ying's survival mentality is typical of all the woman characters who belong to the Joy Luck Club. All the Club Aunties have experienced two kinds of extreme situations: one kind is famine, war, forced marriage, and broken family in China, and the other is cultural alienation, disintegration of old family structure, and conflict between mother and daughter in America. In order to survive the drastic changes in their lives, these women need to maintain a psychological continuity, a coherent picture of life-world, and a continuity of self. Such a need requires the assuring structure of memory narrative: life-story narrative, with the genre's nominal continuity of aims and intentions, and hopes and fears. Memory is for them a socializing, ego-forming expression of anxieties, hopes, and survival instinct.

Indeed, the Joy Luck Club itself, with a magnificent mah jong table at its center, is an expression and embodiment of that survival mentality and its strategies of psychic defense. Suyuan Woo, mother of the book's first narrator, started the first Joy Luck Club in wartime Kweilin as a refugee running away from the triumphantly advancing Japanese troops. In times of trouble, everyday life became an exercise in survival, both physical and mental. If "hero" means someone who takes decisive action during a time of crisis, then for Suyuan Woo, whose life was in crisis, survival itself became a decisive action—a heroic action, albeit a pathetic and disenchanted one. In order to hang on to living, the club members in Kweilin tried to "feast," to "celebrate [their] good fortune, and play with seriousness and think of nothing else but adding to [their] happiness through winning." As Suyuan herself explains:

> It's not that we had no heart or eyes for pain. We were all afraid. We all had our miseries. But to despair was to wish back for something already lost. Or to prolong what was already unbearable.

Suyuan starts the second Joy Luck Club in San Francisco in 1949. This time she is a refugee fleeing from the triumphant Communists in China. This second club is both a memory of the first club and a renewed means of survival. For those new club members newly immigrated to America, "who had unspeakable tragedies they had left behind in China and hopes they couldn't begin to express in their fragile English," the happy moments of playing mah jong are the only time they can "hope to be lucky"— "That hope was our only joy."

If the mah jong club reflects and is part of the Club Aunties' survival endeavor, it is not just a common sense survival that describes the difficulty of making ends meet or alludes to the fear of poverty. It expresses the perception that they are all survivors in the sense that they have lived through dark times and have emerged in the new world. It indicates the urgency to hold one's life together in the face of mounting pressures, which are seen in the dire light reflected from their memories of specific events that once victimized them in earlier times. Understanding is made necessary when one encounters the unfamiliar, the unknown, the uncanny. The process of understanding ordinarily begins with the displacement of the thing unknown toward something that is known, apprehended, and familiar. The process of understanding thus begins with an experiential shift. The domain of the unknown is shifted, by renewing the old strategy of survival, toward a domain or field presumably already mastered. All the stories included in the first section of the book are about mother-narrators' experiences of victimization. These old memories help shift the narrators, especially in an unfamiliar environment, to a growing belief that people are all victimized, in one way or another, by events beyond their control.

However, memories are not one-way tracks, as some early philosophers would like to suggest. If the past casts a shadow on the present through memory, the present also pre-imposes on the past by means of memory. It is worth noting that John Perry, a philosopher who has written widely on the relationship between memory and personal identity, believes that "a sufficient and necessary condition of my having participated in a past event is that I am able to remember it." The one-way track memory is what Nietzsche calls the "inability to forget," a symptom of a sick person who has given in to past failures and discomforts, making the present unbearable and the future hopeless. What we find with the Joy Luck Club mothers is what Nietzsche calls "memory of the will," an active memory that is sustained by the will to survive (Nietzsche "Second Essay"). Suyuan told her refugee story in so many varied ways that her daughter does not know how to relate them to reality and can only take them as "a Chinese fairy tale." These stories, in the form of memory, test Suyuan's ability to forget. These stories are her symptomatic records of a traumatized soul making a desperate effort to push back the memory of the tragic loss of a husband and two baby daughters during the war. The real memory was suppressed but did not go away; and Suyuan, as her second husband feels intuitively, "was killed by her own thoughts," which she could not even articulate to her husband and daughter.

Not only does Suyuan's early experience of extreme situations result in a defensive contraction of self, but also it transforms her relationship with her daughter into one of survival, a fear that she will lose her connection with her daughter, and that her experiences, thoughts, beliefs, and desires will have no future successors. The daughter may look like the mother, or even identify with her; and yet, the two are still worlds apart from each other. Perry makes a very important differentiation between "identification" and "identity," and points out, "Identity is not a necessary condition of identification. I can identify with the participant in events I did not do, and would not do, even if they were to be done." Georges Rey, in his study of the existential unrepeatability of personal experience and identity, emphasizes the impossibility of passing on identity through the narrative of memory:

> There are . . . an alarmingly diverse number of ways in which one person might come to share the seeming memories of another: vivid stories, hallucinations. . . . All my and my grandfather's hopes to the contrary, he does not survive as me, no matter how much I seem to recollect (and even take as my own) the experiences of his life from having heard of them at his knees. This is partly because we were both alive when I heard and identified with them; and, for all our not inconsiderable mutual concern, none of it was (strictly) personal. I didn't thereafter enjoy any privileged access to his feelings and thoughts.

Memory is not just a narrative, even though it does have to take a narrative form; it is more importantly an experiential relation between the past and the present, projecting a future as well. It is the difference of experiential networks between Suyuan Woo and her daughter that accounts for the daughter's resistance to the mother's nagging about hard work and persistence, as well as for her confusion about the mother's constant sense of crisis.

Hard work and persistence are with the mother—and most "diligent" Chinese immigrants—less self-sufficient virtues than means and conditions of survival. These qualities are desirable to her just because she learnt from her previous experiences that they are attributes of a "winner" in life, and she is going to treat them only as such. It is only on the usefulness of these qualities that she will base her self-approval for exercising them. Even though she knows pretty well that her daughter will never get a Ph.D., she keeps telling her friends and neighbors that Jing-mei Woo is working on it. This is less a lie or wishful thinking than an expression of her survival instinct: what the mother seeks from her friends and neighbors is not the kind of approval that applauds her daughter's personal qualities, but the conviction for herself that her daughter possesses the attributes of a survivor.

It is too easy to advance diligence, frugality, or whatever as Chinese ethnic qualities. What is wrong in such a view is an essentialist interpretation of these qualities as inherent "Chinese" attributes, and a blindness to their special relations with a particular kind of ethnic memory.

The disposition for many first generation Chinese immigrants in America to see life as a constant test of survival, to the extent that it almost becomes ethnic symbolism, is a complex mentality. It is deeply rooted in China's past of hardship and numerous famines and wars. The word in Chinese that denotes "making a living in the world" is *qiusheng*—seeking survival, or *mousheng*—managing survival. The Chinese classics are full of wisdom on how to survive, whether it be Taoist escapism, Confucian doctrine of the mean, or Legalist political trickery. The lack of religion and of a systematic belief in an after-life in Chinese culture indicates the preoccupation with the urgency of surviving in the present world. The simultaneous contempt for business (and "the rich") and love of money (in the form of thriftiness) support the view of money not as a measure of success but as a means of survival.

However, survival mentality in China has never become a symbol of nationality and ethnicity. It is part of the living conditions which have remained intact with little change throughout centuries; but it has never been mobilized and turned into what Werner Sollors, in his *The Invention of Ethnicity*, calls "kinship symbolism." Only when a Chinese person is uprooted from his or her own culture and transplanted into an alien one does he or she become aware of the fluidity, proteanness, and insecurity of his or her self. It is not until then that he or she feels the need to define himself or herself by a reference group, or even deliberately manages a certain image or presentation of self using the symbolism of survival. "Ethnicity," as Sollors aptly observes, "is not so much an ancient and deep-seated force surviving from the historical past. . . . It marks an acquired . . . sense of belonging that replaces visible, concrete communities whose kinship symbolism ethnicity may yet mobilize in order to appear more natural." The newly acquired ethnic awareness of being Chinese in America and the sense of urgency about the individual's and the group's preservation and survival register the waning of the old sense of a durable public world, reassuring in its definiteness, continuity, and long-tested survival strategies.

Once the imagery of confinement, insecurity, alienation, and extreme situations takes hold of the imagination of an ethnic group, the temptation to extend this imagery to lesser forms of stress and hardship and to reinterpret every kind of adversity or difference in the light of survival proves almost irresistible. Things as trifling as the Chinese way of playing mah jong, which, according to the mothers in *The Joy Luck Club*, is different from and far superior to the Jewish mah jong, is jealously guarded as a matter of immense significance. The excessive concern with being "genuinely Chinese" announces the abandonment of efforts to adapt to a mixed and heterogeneous society in favor of mere ethnic survival.

Even at the mah jong table people have to face the agony of how to survive. "We used to play mah jong," explains Auntie An-mei to Jing-mei, "winner take all. But the same people were always winning, the same people always losing." This is what life has always been: there has to be someone who is a loser and a victim. But the San Francisco Joy Luck Club Aunties reformulate their mah jong game so that it becomes, symbolically at least, a game with no losers:

> We got smart. Now we can all win and lose equally. We can have stock market luck. And we can play mah jong for fun, just for a few dollars, winner take all. Losers take home leftovers!

The change in the mah jong game may appear insignificant. But it reflects the Club Aunties' view of the loser as a victim who fails to survive, and their belief that one should make every effort to defend oneself against the bruising experience of being a loser, even at a mah jong table. Such a view can alter the way competition and rivalry are experienced. Competition, whether it be in a chess game, in a piano performance, or for a college degree, now centers not so much on the desire to excel as on the struggle to avoid a crushing defeat. A willingness to risk everything in the pursuit of victory gives way to a cautious hoarding of the reserves necessary to sustain life over the long haul. For Lindo Jong, her daughter's chess championship is not just proof of her talent. It is more essentially her attribute of being "lucky" and being a winner. Worldly success has always carried with it a certain poignancy, an awareness that "you can't take it with you"; but among the Chinese, glory is more fleeting than ever, and those who win a game worry incessantly about losing it.

Lindo Jong gives her daughter Waverly her own talisman of luck—"a small tablet of red jade which held the sun's fire"—in order to add to the latter's "invisible strength." Her daughter's chess battle becomes her own battle. But the worry and concern of her subtle survivalism is not appreciated by her daughter, who accuses her mother of using her to show off and trying to take all the credit. Lindo Jong's "all American made" daughter has a hard time understanding why her mother believes that "luck" and "tricks" are more valuable and more important than "skill" and "smartness." "You don't have to be so smart to win chess," Lindo Jong tells her daughter. "It is just tricks."

Waverly Jong feels immobilized by her mother's "sneak attack," and at first completely misses the disenchanted heroic style that underlies the "sneakiness" of her mother's attack. What she fails to see is that her mother's "sneakiness" is meant to prepare her for dealing with the unpredictable, in which she will constantly find herself faced with unstructured situations and the need to survive on her own. In contrast to the American strategies of survival that Waverly has been introduced to (such as upward mobility, security in legal protection, and active individual choice), Lindo Jong's survivalist strategy of "sneakiness" or "trickiness" is miserably nonheroic and shamefully "Chinese." Waverly fears and despises her mother, and resists her mother's teaching. Puzzled by her daughter's reaction, Lindo Jong confesses:

> I couldn't teach her about the Chinese character. How to obey parents and listen to your mother's mind. How not to show your own thoughts, to put your feelings behind your face so you can take advantage of hidden opportunities. Why easy things are not worth pursuing. How to know your own worth and polish it, never flashing it around like a cheap ring. Why Chinese thinking is best.

The wearing of a mask is to Lindo Jong an heroic act—an act necessary for the survival of poor immigrants like herself, who feel "it's hard to keep your Chinese face in America." Wearing a mask means the ability to suppress one's true feelings and emotions—even to deceive—in order to be allowed to live. She is not unaware of the debt that the mask wearer has to pay to human guile; but in her understanding there is no rage that rips the heart, no passion of combat which stresses the heroic deeds of ethnic rebellion. With many Chinese-Americans like Lindo Jong, survivalism has led to a cynical devaluation of heroism, and to a resignation that is tinged with a bitter sense of humor.

When they first arrived in America, Lindo Jong and An-mei Hsu worked in a fortune cookie factory, making Chinese sayings of fortune for American consumption. Lindo Jong was wondering what all this nonsense of Chinese fortunes was about. An-mei explained to her

> "American people think Chinese people write these sayings."
> "But we never say such things!" [Lindo Jong] said. "These things don't make sense. These are not fortunes, they are bad instructions."
> "No, miss," [An-mei] said, laughing, "it is our bad fortune to be here making these and somebody else's bad fortune to pay to get them."

Lindo Jong knows that the Chinese wearing of the mask, just like those Chinese fortunes, can convince many Americans that they know and understand Chinese people. She also has an unusual insight into the risk that the mask wearer can become psychologically dependent upon the mask, even when the mask is not needed. Continued wearing of the mask makes it difficult for the wearer of the mask to be her real self. Maskedness has almost become the ethnic symbolism for Chinese-Americans like Lindo Jong, who thinks like a person of "two faces," being neither American nor Chinese.

In a self-consciously two-faced person like Lindo Jong we find a detached, bemused, ironic observer, who is almost fascinated by the fact that she has not a self that she can claim as "me." The sense of being an observer of one's own situation and that all things are not happening to "me" helps to protect "me" against pain and also to control expressions of outrage or rebellion. Survivors have to learn to see themselves not as free subjects, but rather as the victims of circumstances, be they the current situation or prefixed fate or disposition.

Chinese Taoist culture helps to maintain this kind of victim mentality because it reinforces a passive if not fatalist attitude toward life. The influence of Taoism, in its popularized form, is obvious in how ying-yang-wu-hsing is used by the mothers in *The Joy Luck Club* as a physiotherapy that helps explain why the life of the unlucky people is what it is. In this popularized form of Taoism, human life is a constant struggle for a precarious balance between ying and yang, affected even by the placing of your bedroom mirror or the location of your condominium apartment. Wu-hsing (the five elements: water, fire, wood, metal, and earth), which were conceived by the Taoist masters as five fundamental phases of any process in space-time, become the mystical ingredients that determine every person's character flaw according to one's birth hour. "Too much fire and you had a bad temper. . . . Too much water and you flowed in too many directions."

Rose Hsu Jordan, like her mother, An-mei, has too little wood, and as a consequence, she bends to other people's ideas. Her marriage with Ted breaks down because he is annoyed by her lack of decision. Measured by the Wu-hsing system, none of us has all the five character elements perfectly balanced, and therefore, every one of us is by nature flawed. This view of human imperfection may appear like the Greek idea of tragic flaw. But the Chinese view of character flaw has no interest in any unyielding defiance to fate. The wily Chinese wisdom and belief that heroes do not survive informs the disenchantment with conventional codes of defiance and heroism. While the Greek tragic heroes face their inevitable destruction with dignity and grace, the believers in Wu-hsing want to survive by amending the flaw through non-heroic small acts such as taking "special names" the "rose" in

Rose Hsu Jordan's name, for example, is supposed to add wood to her character.

Both Rose Hsu Jordan and her mother regard themselves as victims of circumstances, but, belonging to two different generations, they resort to different strategies in order to alleviate their fear of disaster. An-mei Hsu copes with everyday mishaps by preparing for the worst and by keeping faith in hope. Her faith in God, which she held for many years before her youngest boy was drowned, was less a religious belief for which she was ready to sacrifice herself than a survival strategy of keeping herself in hope. Although An-mei keeps telling her daughter to make her choice, or even to indulge in a fantasy revenge for the wrongs suffered by women, she is prepared to accept the worst thing that can happen to a woman: the fate of being a woman, "to desire nothing, to swallow other people's misery, to eat my own bitterness."

An-mei's faith in God, or, after the death of her boy, in hope, is to her American-made daughter only a fatalist's self-created illusion. "[My mother] said it was faith that kept all these good things coming our way," Rose Hsu Jordan tells us with her tongue in cheek, "only I thought she said 'fate,' because she couldn't pronounce that 'th' sound in 'faith.'" Rose has to be tempered by her own suffering before she will discover that "maybe it was fate all along, that faith was just an illusion that somehow you're in control."

Instead of relying completely on her mother's advice, Rose, devastated by her broken marriage, goes to her psychiatrist. Psychiatry, for Rose the young Chinese-American, has played the role of modern successor to religion. In psychiatry, the religious relief for souls has given way to "mental hygiene," and the search for salvation to the search for peace of mind. Rose tells her psychiatrist about her fantasy revenge against Ted, and feels like having "raced to the top of a big turning point in my life, a new me after just two weeks of psychotherapy." She expects an illuminating response from her psychiatrist. However, just like her mother was forsaken by God, Rose is let down by her mundane saver "my psychiatrist just looked bored." It is only after her frustrating experience with her psychiatrist that Rose feels an accidental connection of a shared fate between herself and her mother. The mother and daughter are co-victims of a common threatening force over which they have no control. It is when Rose, in her dream, sees her mother planting trees and bushes in the planter boxes, adding wood to both of them, that she lets us get a close view of a mother-daughter relation that is defined neither by blood tie nor by material service, a relation that is neither Chinese nor American, but Chinese-American.

This mother-daughter relationship with a unique ethnic character is what we discern not only in the Hsu family, but also in the families of Woos,

Jongs, and St. Clairs. The family tie between the mother and daughter in each of these Chinese-American families is no longer what determines the Chinese daughter's obligation or the Chinese mother's authority. Family features shared by mother and daughter in those Chinese-American families are not something to be proud of, but rather something that causes embarrassment on one side or the other, and often on both sides. However, neither does this mother-daughter relationship rest, as is common in the American family, on material service. The cross-generation relationship rests on a special service the mother renders to the daughter: the mother prepares the daughter for the extreme situations of life, gives her psychic protection whenever possible, and introduces her to resources she needs to survive on her own. The mother does all this not in the capacity of a self-righteous mother, but as a co-victim who has managed to survive. The traditional role of a Chinese mother has been greatly curtailed in America. If formerly she represented an automatic authority, now she is unsure of herself, defensive, hesitant to impose her own standards on the young. With the mother's role changed, the daughter no longer identifies with her mother or internalizes her authority in the same way as in China, if indeed she recognizes her authority at all.

The loosened family tie and shaky continuity between the two generations represented in *The Joy Luck Club* account for the particular narrative form in which their life acts and events are told. These stories share no apparently recognizable pattern or fully integrated narrative structure. The character relations are suggested but never sufficiently interwoven or acted out as a coherent drama. Our attention is constantly called to the characteristics of fiction that are missing from the book. It is neither a novel nor a group of short stories. It consists of isolated acts and events, which remain scattered and disbanded. It has neither a major plot around which to drape the separate stories, nor a unitary exciting climax which guides the book to a final outcome.

Yet all these customary habitual ingredients have a place in *The Joy Luck Club*. The successions of events are fully timed and narrators of these events are carefully grouped in terms of theme as well as generation distribution (mothers and daughters). The book's sixteen stories are grouped into four sections: the two outer sections are stories by three mother-narrators, and Jing-mei Woo, who takes the place of her recently deceased mother; and the two inner sections are stories by four daughter-narrators. The stories in the first two sections are followed by successive denouements in the next two sections, leading to a series of revelations. All the energies set in motion in the first story of the book, which is told by the book's "framework" narrator, come to fruitful release in the book's last story told by the same narrator, Jing-mei Woo.

Just as the mah jong table is a linkage between the past and present for the Club Aunties, Jing-mei Woo, taking her mother's seat at the table, becomes the frame narrator linking the two generations of American Chinese, who are separated by age and cultural gaps and yet bound together by family ties and a continuity of ethnic heritage. It is Jing-mei Woo who tells the book's two frame stories, the first and the last. These two frame stories, ending with a family reunion in China, suggest strongly a journey of maturity, ethnic awakening, and return-to-home, not just for Jing-mei Woo, but metaphorically for all the daughters in the book. This experience is like a revelation—a sudden unveiling of the authentic meaning of being "Chinese." The ecstatic character of this experience is well expressed by Jing-mei Woo:

> The minute our train leaves the Hong Kong border and enters Shenzhen, China, I feel different. I can feel the skin on my forehead tingling, my blood rushing through a new course. My mother was right. I am becoming Chinese.

At this moment, she seems to come to a sudden realization that to be "Chinese" is a lofty realm of being that transcends all the experiential attributes she once associated with being a Chinese, when she was unable to understand why her mother said that a person born Chinese cannot help but feel and think Chinese:

> And when she said this, I saw myself transforming like a werewolf, a mutant tag of DNA suddenly triggered, replicating itself insidiously into a syndrome, a cluster of telltale Chinese behaviors, all those things my mother did to embarrass me—haggling with store owners, pecking her mouth with a toothpick in public, being color-blind to the fact that lemon yellow and pale pink are not good combinations for winter clothes.
>
> But today I realize I've never really known what it means to be Chinese. I am thirty-six years old. My mother is dead and I am on a train, carrying with me her dreams of coming home. I am going to China.

The book has, for other daughters, other moments of revelation like this one experienced by Jing-mei Woo, though they are of a more subtle nature and of less intensity. It is at these moments of revelation, often after their own sufferings in life, that the daughters come to realize the value and reason of their mothers' survival mentality and the disenchanted heroism of mask and endurance, and begin to hear the rich and multiple meanings in their mothers' stories instead of mere dead echoes of past acts and events. They become less resistant to identifying with their mothers and more receptive to the humble wisdom of the previous generations. The change from resistance to acquiescence signifies simultaneously the growth of a mature self and the ethnicization of experience.

The need to ethnicize their experience and to establish an identity is more real and more perplexing to the daughters than to the mothers, who, after all, are intimate with and secure in their Chinese cultural identity in an experiential sense, in a way their American-born daughters can never be. The daughters, unlike their mothers, are American not by choice, but by birth. Neither the Chinese nor the American culture is equipped to define them except in rather superficial terms. They can identify themselves for sure neither as Chinese nor American. Even when they feel their identity of "Americanness" is an estrangement from their mothers' past, there is no means of recovering the Chinese innocence, of returning to a state which their experiential existence has never allowed them. They are Chinese-Americans whose Chineseness is more meaningful in their relationship to white Americans than in their relationship to the Chinese culture they know little about. The return to their ethnic identity on the part of the daughters is represented in *The Joy Luck Club* as realizable on a level where a real split between the existential self and the ethnic self is alluded to by a narrative rivalry between "tale of the past" and "tale of the present." Not only are the contrast and discontinuity between the two types of tales metaphorical of the split of self, but also their organizing narrator, Jing-mei, is symbolic of the split self of the daughters' generation.

The ethnicization of experience does not automatically mean an ethnic identity. The ethnicized and mature self acquiesces to the ethnic affiliation that fixes its patterns and meanings, but at the very point of acquiescence, registers discomfort with such constraints. Indeed the strange blending of acquiescence and resistance accounts for the fact that the return to the motherland in *The Joy Luck Club* is temporary and disillusioning, no more than a "visit." Such a visit is at once an assertion of "going home" and a painful realization of "going home as a stranger."

Therefore, the significance of the book's frame device of return-to-home and its satisfaction of the reader's formal expectations should not disarm our critical query as to whether the ethnic self really represents a higher form of self or self-awareness. The book's frame device suggests the split between the true but unrecognized self and the false outer being whose sense of self and identity is determined by the need to adjust to the demands of a fundamentally alien society. Such a dualist view of self offers the reassuring but problematic concept of ethnic reality as that which is familiar and recuperated, and which, in the homeland, loyally awaits our return even though we turn from it. It assumes that the "inner" or "true" self is occupied in maintaining its identity by being transcendent, unembodied, and thus never to be discovered until the moment of epiphany. Not only does this cozy view of return to the authentic self suggest a split between the existential self and the ethnic self, but also a fixed hierarchy of them, with the changing and trapped existential self at the bottom, and the essential and free ethnic identity at the top. However, this hierarchy is unstable: the ethnic self, just like the existential self, is neither free nor self-sufficient, and therefore, never an authentic or genuine self. Our ethnic experience, no less than our existential experience, depends on the mediation of others. We become aware of our ethnicity only when we are placed in juxtaposition with others, and when the priority of our other identities, such as individual, class, gender, and religious, give place to that of ethnicity. Like other kinds of identities, ethnic identity is not a fixed nature, or an autonomous, unified, self-generating quality. It is a self-awareness based on differentiation and contextualization. The self is not a given, but a creation; there is no transcendent self, ethnic or whatever else. Ethnic awareness is not a mysteriously inherited quality; it is a measurable facet of our existence, whose conditions and correlates are the only context in which we can understand how we reconstitute feelings and inner knowledge of our own ethnic being.

STEPHEN SOURIS

"Only Two Kinds of Daughters": Inter-Monologue Dialogicity in The Joy Luck Club

"Only two kinds of daughters," she shouted in Chinese. "Those who are obedient and those who follow their own mind! Only one kind of daughter can live in this house. Obedient daughter!"

My mother and I never really understood one another. We translated each other's meanings and I seemed to hear less than what was said, while my mother heard more.

Amy Tan, *The Joy Luck Club*

Amy Tan has said that she never intended *The Joy Luck Club* to be a novel. Instead, she thought of it as a collection of stories. But she did plan on having the stories cohere around a central theme, and she did plan the prefaces from the start, although they were written last. More importantly, her collection of first-person monologues participates in and contributes to a tradition of multiple monologue narratives. Since the precedent-setting experiments of Woolf and Faulkner—*The Waves, The Sound and the Fury, As I Lay Dying, Absalom, Absalom!*—a number of interesting novels written in the decentered, multiple monologue mode have been published. Louise Erdrich's *Tracks*, Peter Matthiessen's *Killing Mister Watson*, Louis Auchincloss's *The House of the Prophet*, and Kaye Gibbons's *A Virtuous*

From *MELUS* Vol. 19, No. 2 (Summer 1994). © 1994 by the Society for the Study of Multi-Ethnic Literature of the U.S.

Woman are just a few of the contemporary examples of this compelling genre.

Because of its decentered, multi-perspectival form, *The Joy Luck Club* invites analysis from critical perspectives that theorize and valorize fragmented, discontinuous texts and the possibilities of connection across segments. Mikhail Bakhtin may come to mind first because of his emphasis on and celebration of texts flaunting a diversity of fully valid and autonomous voices with relativistic and centrifugal consequences as well as counter-centrifugal tendencies such as the active intermingling of perspectives within single consciousnesses (what I call "intra-monologue dialogicity"). Tan's "novel" offers a heteroglot collection of very different, fully valid voices each presented from its own perspective, with relativistic and centrifugal implications. Moreover, its unique theme—mothers from China and their American-born daughters struggling to understand each other—allows for a rich array of dialogized perspectives within single utterances: the Chinese, the American, and the Chinese-American, all three of which can be discerned, to varying degrees, in the monologues.

My concern in this essay, however, will not be with the counter-centrifugal phenomenon of "intra-monologue dialogicity." Rather, it will be with what I call "inter-monologue dialogicity," or the potential for active intermingling of perspectives across utterances, with the site of the dialogicity located in the reader's experience of the narrative. Although Bakhtin has some provocative things to say about the dialogic potential of textual segments set side by side and even hints at the role a reader would have to play in establishing that dialogicity, his theory does not fully allow for a reader's moment-by-moment processing of a text. Wolfgang Iser picks up where Bakhtin leaves off regarding the counter-centrifugal dialogicity that can be said to exist between textual elements in a multiple narrator novel. It is with his narrative model that I propose to uncover and articulate the dialogic potential across monologues in *The Joy Luck Club*.

Iser's phenomenologically rigorous model of the act of reading is ideally suited to the pursuit and articulation of inter-monologue dialogicity in narratives modeled more or less after *The Sound and the Fury*, *As I Lay Dying*, or *The Waves*. Although *The Act of Reading* is a classic text in the reader-response school, a brief summary of the main points of Iser's theory will establish the context for my analysis of the potentially interacting structures of *The Joy Luck Club*.

Like other reader-response critics, Iser emphasizes the active involvement of the reader in the creation of meaning. For Iser, reading is a "dynamic happening" and is the product of a "dyadic interaction" between text and reader. "Meaning is an effect to be experienced," he asserts; it does not inhere in a literary work independent of the reading experience. For Iser, "literary texts initiate 'performances' of meaning rather than actually formulating meanings themselves." Meaning for Iser is "text-guided though reader-produced." What a reader encounters in processing a text are "instructions for the production of the signified."

Iser's emphasis on the reader's active involvement with the text does not allow for the extreme subjectivism that Norman Holland and David Bleich allow for in their theories. As such, Iser's model is relatively conservative because it insists that all concretizations be "intersubjectively" valid: "The subjective processing of a text is generally still accessible to third parties, i.e., available for intersubjective analysis." Indeed, the reason for restricting the creative activity of the reader is to allow for observations that can be agreed upon across subjectivities: "One task of a theory of aesthetic response is to facilitate intersubjective discussion of individual interpretations." To that end, Iser distinguishes between "meaning" and "significance": "meaning" is what all readers who are properly following the "instructions for the production of the signified" should arrive at; "significance" concerns how a particular reader might apply that meaning to his or her own life. But the emphasis in Iser's model is always with the processing of textual elements rather than the production of a detachable message, as he indicates by asserting that "what is important to readers, critics, and authors alike is what literature does and not what it means."

In calling for an "erotics of art" (following Sontag ["Indeterminacy"]), and in inviting the reader to "climb aboard" the text, Iser emphasizes the moment-by-moment experience of what a text "does" to the reader. He refers to the reader's "wandering viewpoint" because of this emphasis on the temporal experience of a text. "The wandering viewpoint," he argues, "divides the text up into interacting structures, and these give rise to a grouping activity that is fundamental to the grasping of a text." These interactive structures are conceptually apprehended as a gestalt. Any perspective of the moment—or "theme," in his terminology—is apprehended against the backdrop of a previous "theme," which becomes the "horizon." For Iser, responding to the textual prompts as "instructions for the production of the signified" amounts to actively recalling previous moments and allowing them to enter into significant combinations with present moments. Or, since his model allows for readers rereading, any present moment can be creatively paired up with a moment one remembers will be encountered later in the text. Constantly creating foreground/background *Gestalten*, an Iserian reader's experience of a text is very three dimensional. But each theme/horizon concretization is temporary and may have to be modified as other *Gestalten* are experienced. Iser expresses this complex concept thusly: "The structure of theme and horizon constitutes the vital

link between text and reader . . . because it actively involves the reader in the
process of synthesizing an assembly of constantly shifting viewpoints, which
not only modify one another, but also influence past and future syntheses in
the reading process." Iser illustrates the concept of constantly modifying
one's concretizations by comparing the reading experience to a cybernetic
feedback loop. Because of this experiential emphasis, he can assert that "the
text can never be grasped as a whole, only as a series of changing viewpoints,
each one restricted in itself and so necessitating further perspectives."

"Gaps" or "blanks" (*Unbestimmtsheitsstellen*) provide the impetus for the
creation of a theme/horizon gestalt by inviting the reader to respond to an
interruption in the flow or exposition with a meaning-creating pairing.
"Wherever there is an abrupt juxtaposition of segments there must
automatically be a blank," he argues, "breaking the expected order of the
text." Iserian gaps have been explained as "conceptual spaces" between
textual elements that allow for reader ideation. According to Iser, "Gaps are
bound to open up, and offer a free play of interpretation for the specific way
in which the various views can be connected with one another. These gaps
give the reader a chance to build his own bridges." But gaps do not really
allow for "free play"; the reader must engage in "intersubjectively" valid
concretizations: "The structured blanks of the text stimulate the process of
ideation to be performed by the reader on terms set by the text." The
concept of *Unbestimmtsheitsstellen*, or gaps, is Iser's central trope for figuring
the active reader involvement required by the reading experience.

The final concept to summarize before applying Iser's
phenomenologically precise model of the reading process to Tan's *Joy Luck
Club* is negativity. For Iser, the depiction of anything unattractive or deformed
automatically causes the reader to imagine a positive counterbalance. This is
another kind of gap, then: deformity creates a space in which the active reader
compensates for the unattractive depiction with the imagining of a more
positive situation or character.

Iser's unusual sensitivity to the moment-by-moment construction of
the text by a reader makes his theory especially relevant to fragmented texts.
Indeed, he "valorizes the discontinuous work" that is full of gaps. This can
be seen in his comments on *Ulysses, The Sound and the Fury*, and *Humphrey
Clinker* in *The Implied Reader* and *The Act of Reading*.

Reading *The Joy Luck Club* in the context of Iser's elaborately worked
out theory and his remarks on fragmented, multi-perspectival texts require
paying attention to the way in which a reader's moment-by-moment
processing of the text confers a centripetal coherence upon a potentially
chaotic, centrifugal collection. We need to ask how the discontinuous nature
of the narrative (the gaps between sections, in particular) impels the reader

to establish *Gestalten* that are multiple, constantly shifting, and thematically suggestive. We need to look for ways in which initial constructions of foreground/background configurations have to be revised as additional text is encountered. And we need to ask where the line can be drawn between responses that are "intersubjectively" valid and those that range beyond what can be agreed upon intersubjectively.

The segmented presentation of *The Joy Luck Club* allows for many combinational possibilities. I will present some of the most salient *Gestalten*; other foreground/background pairings will, no doubt, suggest themselves based on the examples I offer.

One way *Gestalten* can be created is through juxtapositions of contiguous and non-contiguous monologues. With contiguously placed utterances that "speak to" each other, the side-by-side placement of monologues with common denominators, or, to use Bakhtin's term, "semantic convergence," constitutes an overt invitation to the reader to explore the dialogic potential between the monologues. In these cases, the gap between the sections, which always invites a reflective pause, ensures that a rereading reader will make the connection (although the reader still deserves credit for making the connection).

The first cluster of four monologues provides us with some examples of meaningful juxtapositions, both contiguous and non-contiguous.

In the opening monologue of the novel, Jing-mei (June) offers comments on both Ying-ying and An-mei that color our attitude toward those two. Of Ying-ying, she says that the aunt "seems to shrink even more every time I see her." A few pages later, she adds to this unflattering picture by reporting what her mother thought of Ying-ying: "'Oh, I have a story,' says Auntie Ying loudly, startling everybody. Auntie Ying has always been the weird auntie, someone lost in her own world. My mother used to say, 'Auntie Ying is not hard of hearing. She is hard of listening.'" A few monologues later, we meet Ying-ying from her own point of view. Her account of the traumatic experience of falling off her family's boat and, more generally, growing up in a wealthy family without much contact with her mother, sets up a meaningful gestalt with Jing-mei's comments. On first reading, June's unappreciative comments prejudice us against Ying-ying as the "weird" one; when we read her own account of her childhood and pair that with Jing-mei's words, we realize Jing-mei's account is reductive. On the outside she may appear to be shrinking, and she may appear "hard of listening"; on the inside she has a story to tell that helps explain why she is the way she is. The experience of this gestalt, which shifts depending on one's position in the text (June's words as foreground, Ying-ying's monologue as background, or the latter's monologue as foreground, and June's unappreciative words as background), points out to the reader that greater understanding can lead to greater appreciation and tolerance.

June also comments on An-mei in an unappreciative manner, reporting what her mother has said of An-mei. This allows for the establishment of another theme/horizon configuration. "'She's not stupid,' said my mother on one occasion, 'but she has no spine. . . .' 'Auntie An-mei runs this way and that,' said my mother, 'and she doesn't know why.' As I watch Auntie An-mei, I see a short bent woman in her seventies, with a heavy bosom and thin, shapeless legs. She has the flattened soft fingertips of an old woman." When we meet An-mei in "Scar" immediately after June's opening monologue, we realize that her childhood helps explain why she appears to have no spine. Her moving account of her painful separation from her mother and the traumatic circumstances resulting in her throat scar establishes a context for her apparent spinelessness; it adds to the outer appearance of weakness a story that makes the reductive labeling inadequate to the human reality. This juxtaposition would be interesting even if An-mei herself said she did not have spine: the theme/horizon juxtaposition would make for a poignant realization in the reader's mind of the subjective, limited nature of understanding, with An-mei's terrible childhood, on the one hand, helping to explain why she behaves the way she does, and the unsympathetic, reductive pigeonholing by Suyuan, on the other, typifying the overly reductive manner in which we often sum people up.

The theme/horizon gestalt produced and experienced by the reader following the textual prompts is further enhanced, however, when it is remembered that An-mei thinks she herself does have spine, and that her daughter Rose is the one who is weak. Rose tells us in "Without Wood": "My mother once told me why I was so confused all the time. She said I was without wood. Born without wood so that I listened to too many people. She knew this, because once she had almost become this way." June's mother, Suyuan, who was a bold woman, may have thought that An-mei lacked spine; An-mei, who is proud of having stood up for herself after her mother died, thinks that her daughter lacks "wood": what results is a vivid realization in the mind of the reader who is alert to the potential dialogicity between textual segments that some things are entirely relative.

Another kind of inter-monologue dialogicity in the first cluster of four monologues consists of a triptych of personality differences—the monologues of An-mei, Lindo, and Ying-ying. At the center of this trio of self-portraits is a remarkably bold and strong individual who managed to extract herself from a repressive situation cleverly and diplomatically so that everyone benefited. Lindo's resourcefulness and boldness is framed by two portraits of passivity and weakness: An-mei and Ying-ying are victims of their childhood circumstances. As we move from An-mei's "Scar" to Lindo's "Red Candle," we are impressed with the very different responses to repressive circumstances; as we move from Lindo's "Red Candle" to Ying-ying's "Moon Lady" we return to the perspective of a victim. One specific gestalt the reader is invited to create between Lindo's "Red Candle" and Ying-ying's "Moon Lady" revolves around the "semantic convergence" (using Bakhtin's phrase) of losing and finding oneself. Lindo tells us that she discovered her inner power through an epiphany:

> I asked myself, What is true about a person? Would I change in the same way the river changes color but still be the same person? And then I saw the curtains blowing wildly, and outside rain was falling harder, causing everyone to scurry and shout. I smiled. And then I realized it was the first time I could see the power of the wind. I couldn't see the wind itself, but I could see it carried the water that filled the rivers and shaped the countryside. It caused men to yelp and dance.
>
> I wiped my eyes and looked in the mirror. I was surprised at what I saw. I had on a beautiful red dress, but what I saw was even more valuable. I was strong. I was pure. I had genuine thoughts inside that no one could see, that no one could ever take away from me. I was like the wind.
>
> I threw my head back and smiled proudly to myself. And then I draped the large embroidered red scarf over my face and covered these thoughts up. But underneath the scarf I still knew who I was. I made a promise to myself: I would always remember my parents' wishes, but I would never forget myself.

This remarkable passage about self-discovery and self-assertion in the midst of repression can be set in dialogue with the concluding passage in Ying-ying's monologue following Lindo's, where Ying-ying tells us that the most important moment of her childhood was when she lost herself:

> Now that I am old, moving every year closer to the end of my life, I . . . feel closer to the beginning. And I remember everything that happened that day [the day she fell into the water] because it has happened many times in my life. The same innocence, trust, and restlessness, the wonder, fear, and loneliness. How I lost myself.

> I remember all these things. And tonight, on the fifteenth
> day of the eighth moon, I also remember what I asked the
> Moon Lady so long ago. I wished to be found.

These contiguously placed monologues with a common denominator of finding or losing one's self enter into a dialogicity of difference with the reader as the agent and site of the dialogicity. The result is to enhance the range of personalities offered: the mothers, for all their similarities, are indeed very different, as comparisons such as the one just made establish. Tan succeeds in achieving a truly diverse and heteroglot range of mothers' perspectives in *The Joy Luck Club*.

Another example of counter-centrifugal gestalt the reader is invited to create from contiguously placed monologues consists of a pairing of Lena's worries in "Rice Husband" with Waverly's worries in "Four Directions." In this third quartet of monologues, both Lena and Waverly express frustration over their meddlesome mothers. In "Rice Husband," Lena is apprehensive about her mother's visit, fearing that her mother will perceive that her relationship with Harold is flawed. Ying-ying has an unusual ability to sense trouble and even predict calamity.

> During our brief tour of the house, she's already found the
> flaws. . . . And it annoys me that all she sees are the bad parts.
> But then I look around and everything she's said is true. And
> this convinces me she can see what else is going on, between
> Harold and me. She knows what is going to happen to us.

Knowing that there is something wrong with the rigid policy she and Harold follow of sharing all costs equally, she is afraid her mother will confront her with a truth she does not want to admit. Waverly, on the other hand, is worried that her mother will poison her relationship with Rich the way Lindo poisoned her marriage with her previous husband, Marvin. Lindo had effectively ruined the gift of a fur coat Rich had given Waverly: "Looking at the coat in the mirror, I couldn't fend off the strength of her will anymore, her ability to make me see black where there was once white, white where there was once black. The coat looked shabby, an imitation of romance." Lindo has destroyed something that Waverly took pleasure in. Likewise, she is apprehensive that Lindo will undermine her love for Rich.

> I already knew what she would do, how she would be quiet at
> first. Then she would say a word about something small,

something she had noticed, and then another word, and another, each one flung out like a little piece of sand, one from this direction, another from behind, more and more, until his looks, his character, his soul would have eroded away. And even if I recognized her strategy, her sneak attack, I was afraid that some unseen speck of truth would fly into my eye, blur what I was seeing and transform him from the divine man I thought he was into someone quite mundane, mortally wounded with tiresome habits and irritating imperfections.

Whereas Ying-ying will confront Lena with something Lena should deal with, Lindo will insidiously undermine the love Waverly has for Richard, thus poisoning her relationship. The gestalt that the text invites the reader to create from these contiguously placed monologues counters the centrifugal tendency of this decentered text by setting into an aesthetically meaningful dialogue these two very different kinds of apprehension. This linkage across monologues works to point out the difference between the two daughters—thus enhancing the heteroglot nature of the multi-voiced narrative—even as it creates coherence across fragments through the essential similarity.

In Bakhtinian terms, we might think of Lena's and Waverly's apprehensions as entering into a dialogic relationship of similarity. Bakhtin points out in *Problems of Dostoevsky's Poetics* that there can be a dialogicity between two speakers uttering the same words—"Life is good"—depending on the particular nuances each gives to the utterance from embodied and distinct reference points. Simple disagreement can be less dialogic than agreement, he points out. We might say that Lena declares, "Mothers are meddlesome," and that Waverly concurs with "Mothers are meddlesome"; the reader is the agent and the site of the dialogic engagement of these two essentially similar, yet very different, complaints.

My final example of counter-centrifugal *Gestalten* created from contiguously placed monologues is the triptych of three mothers in the final cluster. An-mei's "Magpies," Ying-ying's "Waiting Between the Trees," and Lindo's "Double Face" all present the reader with a mother who wants desperately to reach out and establish a connection with her daughter—in spite of the disagreements and conflicts. Each mother hopes to establish a closer relationship by telling her a story. And each mother is shown with a story to tell. Each mother offers the second installment of her life story: An-mei tells what it was like living with her mother as Fourth Wife; Ying-ying describes her marriage in China, the murder of her child, and her marriage to her current husband; and Lindo tells about how she left China and came to the United States. In each case, however, it appears that the actual communication does not occur. Tan's multiple monologue novel seems to participate in the convention of having speakers speak into the void—or to the reader as audience. No actual communication between mothers and daughters occurs. Presented with these three monologues, the reader is invited to establish the connection between them. The dialogicity of similarity in this gestalt, where each theme of the moment can be set against one or both of the other monologues as the horizon, is a powerfully persuasive method of arguing on behalf of the mothers. No narrative voice need announce that mothers should be listened to; the narrative makes the reader poignantly aware of the distance between each mother and daughter by showing the unbridged gap between them and the potential for sharing and communication that is only partially realized. This triptych of well-meaning mothers who want to pass on something to their daughters is another example of how there can be dialogic potential between similar utterances (as in "Life is good," "Life is good") in a multiple narrator novel, with the reader's consciousness as the site of the inter-monologue dialogicity.

So far, my discussion of the counter-centrifugal *Gestalten* created by the reader has focused on the pairing of "themes" (Iser's term for perspectives of the moment) that are already presented by the narrative in a relationship through simple contiguous juxtaposition. It is also possible to consider *Gestalten* that a reader's wandering viewpoint might create from "themes" that are not already set side-by-side. These juxtapositions might be called conceptual rather than contiguous (although even with side-by-side placement, the resulting gestalt must be a creation in the reader's mind and thus conceptual).

The pairings possible with monologues from Lena and Ying-ying are examples of the interesting *Gestalten* creatable from non-contiguous monologues. We might take Lena's "The Voice from the Wall" as a starting point. Her perspective on her mother is entirely unappreciative here; she has no understanding or sympathy—and how could she, since Ying-ying's past is never talked about ("My mother never talked about her life in China, but my father said he saved her from a terrible life there, some tragedy she could not speak about"). She presents her mother as psychologically imbalanced. She thinks of her mother as a "Displaced Person," using a photograph taken after the scared woman was released from Angel Island Immigration Station to represent her personality:

> In this picture you can see why my mother looks displaced. She
> is clutching a large clam-shaped bag, as though someone might

steal this from her as well if she is less watchful. She has on an ankle-length Chinese dress. . . . In this outfit she looks as if she were neither coming from nor going to someplace. . . .

My mother often looked this way, waiting for something to happen, wearing this scared look. Only later she lost the struggle to keep her eyes open.

We realize that Ying-ying's troubled mental state must have impinged negatively on Lena as she grew up, and we sympathize with her for that. But as readers who are privileged to know the inner thoughts of every character, we can balance off that perspective with what we know from Ying-ying's "Moon Lady" monologue, where we learn about the childhood trauma that has clearly affected her personality. And from "The Voice from the Wall," we can look forward, as well, and set Lena's frustration with her mother's aberrational personality against "Waiting Between the Trees": in this moving monologue, Ying-ying reveals a side of herself that Lena would be surprised to learn about. The Ying-ying we meet here is completely unknown to her daughter:

So I will tell Lena of my shame. That I was rich and pretty. I was too good for any one man. That I became abandoned goods. I will tell her that at eighteen the prettiness drained from my cheeks. That I thought of throwing myself in the lake like the other ladies of shame. And I will tell her of the baby I killed because I came to hate this man so much.

I took this baby from my womb before it could be born. This was not a bad thing to do in China back then, to kill a baby before it is born. But even then, I thought it was bad, because my body flowed with terrible revenge as the juices of this man's firstborn son poured from me.

When the nurses asked what they should do with the lifeless baby, I hurled a newspaper at them and said to wrap it like a fish and throw it in the lake. My daughter thinks I do not know what it means to not want a baby.

When my daughter looks at me, she sees a small old lady. That is because she sees only with her outside eyes. She has no *chuming*, no inside knowing of things. If she had *chuming*, she would see a tiger lady. And she would have careful fear.

This set of *Gestalten*—"Voices" and "Moon Lady," "Voices" and "Waiting"—

points out the relativity theme that this multiple narrator novel, like many, proposes. The very structure and narrative mode of the novel suggest that we appreciate the subjective nature of perception: there is Lena's thinking of her mother as a Displaced Person and Ying-ying's thinking of herself as a "Tiger Woman." However, *The Joy Luck Club* differs from other radically decentered multiple narrator novels—such as *As I Lay Dying* and, more recently, Auchincloss's *The House of the Prophet* or Matthiessen's *Killing Mister Watson*—in that it does not insist on absolute epistemological relativism: the reader who actively pairs momentary "themes" realizes that there is more to Ying-ying than Lena's "Displaced Person" label allows for; the reader senses the potential for dialogue between mother and daughter that fails to take place.

This repeated failure for mother and daughter to enter into meaningful exchange is effectively represented through another Lena/ Ying-ying gestalt: the pairing of Lena's "Rice Husband" monologue with Ying-ying's "Waiting Between the Trees." In "Waiting," Ying-ying is apparently about to cause the unstable table to fall, sending the vase crashing to the floor. She hopes to attract her daughter's attention and get her to come into the room where Ying-ying can talk to her. Ying-ying clearly wants to use it as the occasion to tell Lena everything she has wanted to tell her and to pass on her *chi* to her daughter. But in "Rice Husband," five monologues prior to "Waiting," the vase has already crashed to the floor and mother and daughter have already had their moment together. From what Lena reports in "Rice Husband," nothing came of the encounter. Tan's use of the unstable table as a common denominator across the two monologues constitutes an effective exercise in triangulation, a common technique in multiple narrator novels to demonstrate (usually) the subjective nature of perception.

Another example of triangulation that prompts the reader to create a gestalt pairing two monologues that have a common denominator occurs with An-mei's "Magpies" and Rose's "Without Wood." The common denominator inviting a pairing of the monologues is Rose's psychiatrist. This gestalt is an especially interesting one for the novel because of the way it foregrounds the distance between the traditionally minded Chinese mother living in the United States and the American-born daughter who has embraced many American ways. From the American perspective, it is normal and even stylish for Rose to see a psychiatrist; from the Chinese perspective, seeing a psychiatrist is incomprehensible—indeed, An-mei might even regard it as bringing shame upon the family. An-mei's "Magpies" begins and ends with her complete dismissal of the idea of seeing a psychiatrist; she does not approve of Rose's seeing one. But this conceptual gestalt—"Without Wood" and "Magpies" on the issue of seeing a psychiatrist—is more interesting than just the representation of complete lack of understanding on the part of mother and daughter: Rose actually does stop seeing her shrink—and she's better off because of it. She stops talking to other people as well, which her mother recommended. After a prolonged period of isolation and sleep—three days—she emerges defiant, ready to take on Ted. She thus relies on her own inner strength and faces up to Ted, which is just what her mother wanted her to do. However, she reaches this point on her own, not by simply listening to her mother (her mother's alternative to seeing a psychiatrist is the daughter simply listening to the mother's advice). And confronting Ted seems to have unleashed a realization at a deeper, psychic level about the abusive nature of her mother, as well. In her dream, her mother is planting weeds in her garden that are running wild.

Another example of how non-contiguous "themes" can be set into a gestalt through the active memory and conceptual pairing activity of an Iserian reader is the linkage of the moments of self-assertion throughout the novel. This involves a series of linkages, with several possible pairings, or even one mega-gestalt. Rose's self assertion in "Without Wood" can be linked up with June's in "Two Kinds", An-mei's in "Magpies" (where her self-assertion after the death of her mother is described), and Lindo's in "The Red Candle" (where she describes the epiphany that led her to her ruse, as previously discussed). Here we have another example of the dialogic potential of similar utterances: each of these women has had to assert herself in the face of some kind of oppression; in spite of their differences, they are united on this theme, but each has a different nuance to give to the statement, "I have had to assert myself."

Another way in which *The Joy Luck Club* invites through its discontinuous form the creative work of a reader pairing segments into order—conferring *Gestalten* in response to textual prompts—is with the four prefaces. They serve, much like the interludes in *The Waves*, as a universalizing backdrop against which to see the particularized monologues. Each monologue can be set against the preface, and each cluster can be taken as an Iserian "theme" set against the "horizon" of the respective preface. The prefaces also help the reader pick up on what Tan calls the "emotional curve" of each "quartet" ("Address").

The prelude to Part One, "Feathers From a Thousand *Li* Away," presents in fable-like form a nameless Chinese woman who emigrated to America with hopes that she'd have a daughter who would lead a better life than was possible for a woman in China. The Chinese woman is full of good intentions and hopes for that daughter. But her relationship with her daughter is characterized by distance and lack of communication. The following four monologues reveal mothers who bemoan the distance to their daughters but who had good intentions. This prefatory piece, then, helps us organize the four very different opening monologues around that "emotional curve," which serves as a horizon against which the monologues can be apprehended.

The preface to Part Two, "The Twenty-Six Malignant Gates," helps organize the way we think about the daughters' monologues in that section by suggesting that Chinese mothers can be overbearing in their attempts to protect and control their daughters, and that this will result in rebelliousness on the part of their daughters, as well as misfortune. This brief fable-like anecdote manages to encapsulate the dynamics of the monologues that follow and helps us organize the disparate elements of those monologues around the implied criticism of overprotective, overbearing mothers. If the first preface prepares us to be sympathetic towards the mothers, this second preface prepares us to be sympathetic towards the daughters as we read each monologue against that preface as a backdrop.

The preface to Part Three, "American Translation," also enters into a dialogic relationship with the monologues of that section through the gestalt-producing activity of the reader. Introducing another round of daughters' monologues, it presents us with a mother who appears to be overbearing in her desire for a grandchild. She insists that her daughter mount a mirror on the wall for good luck. The mother sees her grandchild in the mirror; the daughter sees only "her own reflection looking back at her." Tan seems to be suggesting with this the theme of conflicting perspectives and the struggle between daughters and mothers—a theme that is seen in the monologues that follow. Mothers see one thing; daughters see something entirely different. But the metaphor here is actually relevant only to the daughters's perspective: it suggests that mothers project their own subjective preferences upon what they see whereas daughters see objectively, which is itself a distorted notion. From the mothers's perspective, they see clearly and daughters distort reality. Because this preface is designed to make us sympathetic to the daughters, it is slanted towards them; the "emotional curve" is with the daughters.

A dialogic relationship also exists between the final fable-like preface and the final four monologues when the gestalt-creating capacity of the reader is called upon. The preface gives shape to the monologues that follow by presenting a mother who has a grandchild and who is treated sympathetically: she is self-critical and hopeful for her daughter, wishing that her daughter can learn "how to lose [her] innocence but not her hope." Very sympathetic to the mother, this preface prepares us to organize the monologues we are about to encounter in a manner that is sympathetic to the mothers. Reading each monologue in this cluster against the backdrop of the fourth preface helps establish the thematic point.

The *Gestalten* the reader creates from the four prefatory pieces thus confer considerable order upon what might at first appear to be a dizzying display of very different personalities, even with the common denominator of Chinese mothers and Chinese-American daughters. Like *The Waves*, *The Joy Luck Club* sets monologues against third-person interludes that function by suggesting a universal backdrop to the series of individualized voices; unlike *The Waves*, however, which uses nature as the universal backdrop, *The Joy Luck Club* prefaces use nameless human figures and abstract situations to suggest general truths.

Although the narrative invites the reader to establish all sorts of specific pairings between contiguous and non-contiguous monologues, the fundamental *Gestalten*, of course, consist of pairings of mothers collectively and daughters collectively. The daughters complaining about their mothers can be gathered together as one gestalt, with each daughter set against another daughter or the rest of the daughters. Presenting the daughters together in the middle two quartets encourages this kind of pairing. The mothers complaining about their daughters can be gathered together as well, with each complaining mother set against any other or the group. The narrative's most basic gestalt is that of mothers apprehended against the backdrop of daughters, or daughters apprehended against the backdrop of mothers. Among the daughters and among the mothers there is a dialogicity of sameness that consists of a fundamental similarity with individual nuances.

The narrative steers the reader, however, towards a particular kind of gestalt consisting of mothers' and daughters' perspectives; we have more than just an array of different perspectives with combinational possibilities among them. The daughters' positions, however understandable and valid, are enclosed and framed by the mothers' positions; however unreasonable or narrow-minded the mothers may seem in their attempts to impose their wills on their daughters, the narrative's structure, which invites the reader to apprehend the daughters against the backdrop of mothers, gives the mothers the upper hand in the argument. The three mothers presented before Jing-mei's closing monologue acquire a critical mass; their voices add up to an overwhelming appeal to respect the life experience and wishes of the mothers. Amy Ling's observation that the book "more often takes a sympathetic stand toward the mother" is a sound assessment because of the shape Tan gives the collection by allowing the mothers to have the final say.

The reader's processing of the four quartets over time necessitates changing initial assessments and thus illustrates Iser's concept of reading as a feedback loop requiring the revision of *Gestalten*. The Iserian reader's primary activity and response consists of creatively pairing different sections or moments into meaningful *Gestalten* and then revising initial constructions when new material is encountered. The clustering of monologues into quartets tempts the reader into certain judgments that must be revised as more of the text is encountered (upon an initial reading): the first cluster biases us towards the parents; the second and third clusters make us more sympathetic to the daughters; the final cluster ensures that the mothers get the upper hand in the debate, even though the daughters are given a very full hearing. The various foreground/background conceptual structures (and *Gestalten* from contiguously placed monologues are conceptual as well as *Gestalten* from non-contiguous monologues) can be created during an initial reading, or upon rereading (which allows one to reach forward as well as backwards from any present moment of reading).

Iser's concept of negativity, another kind of "gap," also applies to *The Joy Luck Club*. The reader is poignantly aware of the potential for greater communication and understanding, but only in the reader's mind is the dialogicity between positions uncovered and experienced. The mothers and daughters are speaking into a void, not to each other (I read the occasional use of the second person in some of the monologues as an aside to an imagined audience, not an actual audience). Thus the narrative form and the thematic point complement each other. The result of this depiction of failed communication is that the reader, through the process of "negativity," is motivated to imagine a healthier response. Although the narrative provides a solution to the dilemma in the final chapter, the reader's experience before the final chapter of the failure to communicate ensures that the reader will be motivated to avoid such incommunicative relationships in his or her own life.

At this point I would like to address the issue of closure in *The Joy Luck Club*. Although depicting in the final chapter an answer to the problem of non-communication demonstrated up to the ending may seem like the perfect way for Tan to conclude, I have had difficulty accepting what seemed to me to be an overly sentimental and facile resolution. I would like to present my initial assessment of this issue and then attempt to move beyond that resisting response with a more accepting reading of the ending. My purpose in presenting my own experience with the issue of closure in *The Joy Luck Club* is to foreground various issues that I believe are important for an understanding of Tan's book.

In my 1992 study of contemporary American multiple narrator novels, I summed up my discomfort with June's novel-ending monologue thusly:

My sense, when viewing *The Joy Luck Club* in the context of other multiple narrator novels, is that the book is at odds with itself. The various monologues of mothers and daughters, monologues that foreground difference—indeed, that flaunt discrepancy, conflict and relativism—set in motion a centrifugality that cannot so easily be overcome. The happy ending . . . [is] not true to the heteroglot diversity actually revealed throughout the text. . . . In my experience of *The Joy Luck Club*, the Suyuan/Jing-mei reconciliation is not convincing, and there clearly is no final reconciliation between all the mothers and daughters. Thus, as I see it, the attempt to reign in the heteroglossia does not do justice to the resonating diversity; that diversity actually eludes subduing through the kind of reductive thematic reading [that the ending invites].

I then pointed out the similarity between my observation about closure in *The Joy Luck Club* and Dale Bauer's comment about the novels she analyzes in her *Feminist Dialogics*. In Bauer's Bakhtin-inspired uncovering of repressed heteroglossia, she observes that "while the plot resolutions give closure to the novels, the dialogue resists that closure." I continued my attempt to articulate my discomfort with the ending by arguing that the process Iser terms "negativity" is sufficient to make the thematic point without a heavy-handed ending.

The reader's sense of the poignancy inherent in a situation where mothers and daughters do not communicate as fully as they might in itself implies a remedy, in itself motivates the reader to imagine a solution—one that would accommodate the needs of both mothers and daughters. . . . *The Joy Luck Club* interferes with the imagined affirmation by prodding the reader too much. It is one thing to show Waverly, at the close of "Four Directions," attempting to impose an artificial, superficial pleasantness on her deeply problematic relationship with her mother by thinking about taking her mother with her on her honeymoon: that reveals an interesting split within this particular consciousness; it is another matter to have Tan . . . [impose] a superficial sense of harmony at the end of the book that does not do justice to the actual diversity and conflict between the covers. The collection of stories is full of moral potential without the heavy-handed ending simply through its presentation of multiple voices, artistically organized.

My having been immersed in Bakhtin, Iser, and Faulkner at the time contributed to my lack of appreciation for the way this novel ends. Bakhtin's take on the novel as a genre is one that privileges the flaunting of diverse perspectives that, while dialogized, are never resolved into harmonious agreement or simple synthesis. His insistence on "unfinalizability" led me to privilege open-ended multiple narrator novels over those with strong closure. Iser's model led me to privilege texts that allow the reader to establish the thematic point without having it boldly announced. And my reading of Faulkner's own multiple narrator novels likewise biased me. *As I Lay Dying*, for example, while providing a sense of ending, flaunts diversity and discrepancy across subjectivities; it revels in the diverse viewpoints and the isolated personalities. *The Sound and the Fury*, too, while offering closure, resists its own ending and the thematic answer it provides (through Dilsey) to the problem of the solipsistic ego epitomized by the Quentin and Jason monologues. Faulkner, as I read him, is more interested in the poetic potential of pathology than in offering any thematic proposition about life.

My effort to rethink my initial response to the strong sense of closure in *The Joy Luck Club* involves a number of considerations based on feedback about this response from other scholars and my own students.

One of those considerations is gender. The "sentimental" ending of the novel may simply evoke different responses from male and female readers. With the kind of psychodynamic model of personality development that feminists like Nancy Chodorow offer (c.f. *The Reproduction of Mothering*), it is possible to argue that women, who are more oriented to bonding and relationships than men (men emphasize separation and autonomy instead, according to this theory), are less likely to resist Tan's ending. My experience teaching the novel in an all-female classroom at Texas Woman's University was enlightening because no one found the ending to be sentimental or false.

Perhaps the most useful approach to the issue of closure in *The Joy Luck Club* is a culturally grounded one. When Tan's contribution to the multiple narrator sub-genre is considered in the context of Asian values, the desire for an ending that brings the resonating diversity and conflicting positions to a tidy close is entirely understandable.

A culturally nuanced reading of the novel might begin with the fundamental orientation toward the group rather than the individual in Asian cultures generally, as stated in the following passage taken from the classic reference book cited earlier of Asian culture for American therapists whose client population includes Asian Americans:

> American society has tended toward the ideals of the self-sufficient, self-reliant individual who is the master of his or her

fate and chooses his or her own destiny. High value is placed on the ability to stand on your own two feet, or pull yourself up by your own bootstraps, or do your own thing. In contrast, Asian philosophies tend toward an acknowledgment that individuals become what they are because of the efforts of many things and many people. They are the products of their relationship to nature and other people. Thus, heavy emphasis is placed on the nature of the relationship among people, generally with the aim of maintaining harmony through proper conduct and attitudes.

This general orientation toward the group is manifested in the emphasis on respecting and serving one's parents, not resisting them. "The greatest obligation of East Asians," according to McGoldrick and her colleagues, "is to their parents, who have brought them into the world and have cared for them when they were helpless. The debt that is owed can never be truly repaid; and no matter what parents may do the child is still obligated to give respect and obedience"—an attitude that can be traced back to Confucius.

Another aspect of Asian cultures generally (East Asian in this particular case) that is pertinent to a culturally nuanced response to *The Joy Luck Club* has to do with shaming. McGoldrick and her co-authors explain that in these cultures, "shame and shaming are the mechanisms that traditionally help reinforce societal expectations and proper behavior." Vacc and his colleagues explain more specifically that "control of the children [in Chinese and Japanese families] is maintained by fostering feelings of shame and guilt." Without knowing this, it is more likely that the shaming behavior some of the mothers of *The Joy Luck Club* engage in to control their children will result in a reading that blames those mothers for inappropriate behavior. As a consequence of the misunderstanding, such a reader would not grant those mothers the sympathy for which they qualify.

Yet another aspect of Asian culture that contributes to a sensitive reading of Tan's novel is the close relationship between a mother and her children in Asian countries. McGoldrick and her co-authors explain it thusly:

The traditional role of the mother must also be understood and respected within the context of her role expectations within the family. Issues involving the children reflect upon her self-esteem as a mother. We must remember that in the traditional family, the children are primarily her responsibility, as well as her resource for the future. Frequently, issues around perceived dependence of children and overprotection of the mother are raised by American therapists who are unfamiliar with traditional family dynamics of Asian families. Therapists do not always understand that within the family mutual interdependence is stressed and expected. This is not to say that individuation does not occur or is not promoted, but it is constantly tinged with the subconscious knowledge of the relationships and obligations between the individual and other family members.

Although *The Joy Luck Club* gives equal time to the position of daughters who resist or resent a domineering mother, an American reader is less likely to grant those mothers their due without understanding that Asian mothers normally behave in a more heavy-handed manner than their American counterparts.

The final point I wish to make about Asian cultures that contributes to a balanced response to both the mothers and the daughters in *The Joy Luck Club* is that Asian families in America tend to place extraordinary emphasis on the importance of education for their children. Vacc and his co-authors explain it thusly:

> The pressure to succeed academically among Asians is very strong. From early childhood, outstanding achievement is emphasized because it is a source of pride for the entire family. . . . Reflecting the emphasis on education is the finding that college enrollment rates for Chinese and Japanese between the ages of 18 and 24 and the percentage completing college is higher than for any other group in the United States. Parental expectations for achievement can be an additional stress factor in young Asian-Americans.

This information is important for a sensitive response to both Jing-mei and Suyuan, who calls her daughter a "college drop-off." It is in the context of explaining her dropping out of college that Jing-mei tells us: "My mother and I never really understood one another. We translated each other's meanings and I seemed to hear less than what was said, while my mother heard more."

With this background information in mind, it is easier to understand the thematic readings of Tan's novel that do not focus on the differences between mothers and the differences between daughters as much as upon the similarities. In this culture-specific context, Tan's attempt to rein in the reverberating heteroglossia has a compelling logic.

The readings of *The Joy Luck Club* offered by Amy Ling and Elaine Kim are undertaken within this context. They emphasize the mother/daughter gestalt discussed earlier and the importance of the broader dynamic between mothers and daughters that this gestalt suggests; Ling and Kim are not as focused on individual personalities as a reader coming from Faulkner, Bakhtin, and Iser would be. Ling argues that "though the mothers all have different names and individual stories, they seem interchangeable in that the role of mother supersedes all other roles and is performed with the utmost seriousness and determination. All the mothers in *The Joy Luck Club* are strong, powerful women." Kim likewise argues that "one of the triumphs of the book is that it is easy to lose track of the individual women's voices: the reader might turn distractedly to the table of contents, trying to pair the mothers and daughters or to differentiate among them, only to discover the point that none of this matters in the least." Ling's reading privileges the mothers' perspectives and argues that the narrative endorses their position more than the daughters' resisting positions. Her reading of the novel is that it "more often takes a sympathetic stand toward the mother." Ling further argues that in spite of the battles described, the daughters eventually acquiesce: "The daughters' battles for independence from powerful commanding mothers is fierce, but eventually, as in [*The Woman Warrior*], a reconciliation is reached. The daughters realize that the mothers have always had the daughters' own best interests at heart." Ling has no problem with Jing-mei's "act of filial obedience" closing the narrative. Her concluding remarks clearly indicate her acceptance of the ending as a perfectly appropriate one; she does not resist the narrative's attempt to counterbalance the conflicting voices with its ending: "[The novel] ends on a note of resolution and reconciliation. The struggles, the battles, are over, and when the dust settles what was formerly considered a hated bondage is revealed to be a cherished bond." Thematizing the novel, she interprets its message thusly:

> To be truly mature, to achieve a balance in the between-world condition then . . . one cannot cling solely to the new American ways and reject the old Chinese ways, for that is the way of the child. One must reconcile the two and make one's peace with the old. If the old ways cannot be incorporated into the new life, if they do not "mix" as Lindo Jong put it, then they must nonetheless be respected and preserved in the pictures on one's walls, in the memories in one's head, in the stories that one writes down.

Bonnie TuSmith, in her recent study of the importance of community in American ethnic literatures, *All My Relatives* (1993), offers a reading of the battling positions of the narrative that also privileges the mothers' perspective. She interprets the passage describing the Polaroid shot of the three sisters as follows: "This composite image of three daughters who, together, make up one mother reflects the novel's communal subtext, which works as a counterpoint to the textual surface of individualistic strife between mothers and daughters." More specifically, she suggests that the narrative argues against the daughters' individualistic voices and for the establishment of harmony with the mothers:

> The novel opens with Jing-Mei's assuming her mother's role at the mah-jongg table of the Joy Luck Club. Her "substitute" role is recalled in the conclusion when she is in China and taking her mother's place once again. This literary frame alone suggests that, although the mother-daughter power struggle appears individualistic on the surface, there is a different message embedded in the text.

The culturally based, heavily thematic readings that TuSmith and Ling offer thus emphasize the overall *Gestalten* of mothers set against daughters and daughters set against mothers with a nod towards the position of the mothers. Ling emphasizes the importance of the daughters respecting and acknowledging the position of the mothers; TuSmith offers a more complex surface versus deep structure analysis that sees the conflicting perspectives as merely a surface phenomenon and the difference-transcending communalism as a more fundamental underlying impulse.

Although my own earlier reading was not sufficiently cognizant of cultural factors—such as the emphasis in Chinese-American cultures on group and family orientation, respect for parents, shaming by parents for control of children, dependent relationships, and education of children—a reading of *The Joy Luck Club* that fully accounts for its complexity perhaps requires taking a middle-ground position: the narrative, with its overall structure (framing) and thematic conclusion, suggests resolution and reconciliation, but the actual collection of voices cannot with complete accuracy be reduced to a thematic reading. If one imagines Tan writing with her mother looking on (and from what she has said about her relationship with her mother, this seems accurate ["Address"]), there should be no surprise that the novel argues for something while at the same time resisting it through the very presentation of a heteroglot array of individual voices.

In either case, a Bakhtin-inspired and Iser-based reading of *The Joy Luck Club* is possible and contributes to a moment-by-moment uncovering and articulation of the counter-centrifugal dialogicity in the collection of monologues. An Iserian reading locates the various points of difference and agreement across monologues and establishes the connections between them. As Bakhtin suggests, the dialogicity can be of agreement as well as disagreement; to use his example, "Life is good" and "Life is good" can resonate through slightly different accents given to the basic proposition. "Mothers are oppressive" and "Mothers are oppressive"—or "daughters should show respect" and "daughters should show respect"—can likewise resonate across monologues by having a different accentuation with each speaker.

Whether or not one agrees that the novel genuinely achieves a resolution and reconciliation (that might be an objective "meaning" versus subjective "significance" issue, in Iserian terms), an Iserian reading focuses on the moment-by-moment experience of the dialogicity of difference and agreement across monologues. On a first reading, during a rereading, or standing back after reading and selectively meditating on the assemblage, there are several ways the segments enter into a dialogic relationship through the active agency of the reader responding in a controlled way to textual prompts. Meaningful connections can be established between: contiguous monologues, non-contiguous monologues, moments within monologues or entire monologues, prefaces and post-preface monologues, and quartets (such as the mothers' quartets framing the daughters' quartets). We might say that the fundamental Iserian gap in this text is the conceptual space between daughters and mothers, between one generation and the other. The primary objective "meaning" that obtains at the site of the dialogicity—the reader's consciousness—is one of unrealized potential. That, in itself, argues, through Iserian negativity, for children and parents to try to listen better and communicate more. By writing a multiple narrator novel with an argumentative edge to it—a thematic thrust that extends beyond an assertion of the relativity of perception—Tan makes a distinct contribution to the genre of the multiple first-person monologue novel.

VICTORIA CHEN

Chinese American Women, Language, and Moving Subjectivity

To imagine a language means to imagine a form of life.

Wittgenstein, *Philosophical Investigations*

Philosophical Investigations

It was not until the 1970s that Asian American literature became recognized as a separate canon and a "new tradition" of writing. While this "new" form of expression created a new political consciousness and identity, the images and stories that abound in pioneer literature such as Maxine Hong Kingston's *The Woman Warrior* and *China Men* are paradoxically located in "recovered" ethnic history. More recently, Amy Tan's *The Joy Luck Club* also takes the reader through a journey back to a specific set of ethnic memories as the mothers in the stories interweave their experiences struggling for survival and dignity in China and for coherence and hope in America. Part of the reason for the celebration of Asian American women's literature is that it provides an alternative way to think about issues such as language, subjectivity, cultural voice, and ethnic/gender identity.

For Chinese American women such as Kingston, Tan, and the female characters in *The Joy Luck Club*, speaking in a double voice and living in a bicultural world characterize their dual cultural enmeshment. While striving

From *Women & Language* Vol. 18, No. 1 (Spring 1995). © 1995 by *Women & Language*.

to maintain a relationship with their Chinese immigrant parents, the Chinese American daughters also live in a society where one is expected to speak in a "standard" form of English and to "succeed" in the middle class Euro-American way. For Kingston and Tan, writing about their immigrant mothers' neglected pasts and their own tumultuous presents becomes a powerful way to recreate their own identities as Chinese Americans and to confront the dilemma of living biculturally in a society that insists on a homogeneous identity. If a language indeed is intrinsically connected with a form of life, and speaking and writing in a given language necessitates one to participate in that cultural world, how then do these Chinese American women authors position themselves in linguistic/cultural borderlands through the use of language? What are some forms of language and life that make their storytelling possible and intelligible? How do different languages function in their own lives and in their storytelling? How do they use languages to interweave and mediate their multiple identities? This essay attempts to address some of these issues. I will draw upon essays written by and about Kingston and Tan as well as narratives from *The Joy Luck Club* and *The Woman Warrior* in my discussion.

Amy Tan (1991) in her essay "Mother Tongue" discusses that as someone who has always loved language, she celebrates using "all the Englishes I grew up with" in her living and her writing. The English that she hears from her mother, despite its "imperfection," has become their "language of intimacy, a different sort of English that relates to family talk, the language I grew up with." There is a discrepancy, both linguistically and culturally, between the "standard" English that she learns from school and uses in her professional world and the "simple" and "broken" English that is used in her interaction with her mother. However, as Tan points out, speaking her mother's version of English gives her bicultural insight and strength, and she sees the beauty and wisdom in her mother's language: "Her language, as I hear it, is vivid, direct, full of observation and imagery"; "I wanted to capture what language ability tests can never reveal: her intent, her passion, her imagery, the rhythms of her speech and the nature of her thoughts." Kingston also grew up in two languages, her family's Chinese dialect and the public American English in which she was educated. *The Woman Warrior* reveals the disjunction that Kingston experienced in moving between these two languages. While her mother marked her growing up with stories of nameless Chinese women, multiple cultural ghosts, Kingston wrote, "To make my waking life American-normal . . . I push the deformed into my dreams, which are in Chinese, the language of impossible stories." The entire book is devoted to Kingston's ongoing struggle to enter the Chinese cultural world composed of impossible stories and to figure out what it meant to be a Chinese American woman in this society.

Tan's *The Joy Luck Club* is a segmented novel, set in San Francisco in the 1980s, powerfully blending the voices of four Chinese immigrant mothers and their American-born daughters. The book opens with a story of a swan and a woman sailing across an ocean toward America saying, "In America I will have a daughter just like me. But over there . . . nobody will look down on her, because I will make her speak only perfect American English. And over there she will always be too full to swallow any sorrow! She will know my meaning. . . ." The tale symbolizes not only the geographic separation from the woman's motherland but also the alienation later felt by both the mother and daughter in America. The woman's desire for her daughter to speak perfect American English foregrounds the problems and difficulties of communicating and translating between the different languages that they speak. The American dream eventually eludes the immigrant woman beyond her best intentions. Mastering this imaginary perfect English for the American-born daughter turns out not to be a simple ticket to American success. This linguistic competency, ironically, signifies her departure from her mother (and her motherland), deepening the chasm between generations and cultures. Moreover, learning to speak perfect American English may also entail the complex journey of "successful" acculturation which often masks the racism and sexism that belie the American dream.

Although Tan's essay celebrates the two Englishes with which she grew up, and that dual languages and cultures can indeed enrich and enlighten one's life, coherence and double voice do not always come without personal struggle and emotional trauma. As we enter the hyphenated world of the "Chinese-American" women in *The Joy Luck Club*, much of the mothers' and daughters' conversations seem to be focused on debating, negotiating, and wandering between the two disparate cultural logics. Lindo shared her daughters concern that she cannot say whether her Chinese or American face is better: "I think about our two faces. I think about my intentions. Which one is American? Which one is Chinese? Which one is better? If you show one, you must always sacrifice the other." Tan (1990), in her essay "The Language of Discretion," pointed out a special kind of double bind attached to knowing two languages and vehemently rebelled against seeing cultural descriptions as dichotomous categories: "It's dangerous business, this sorting out of language and behavior. Which one is English? Which is Chinese? . . . Reject them all!" "Having listened to both Chinese and English, I also tend to be suspicious of any comparisons between Chinese and English languages." Tan argued: "Typically, one language—that of the person doing the comparing—is often used as the standard, the benchmark for a logical form of explanation."

Speaking a language is inherently political. In the case of Chinese American women, while straddling and juggling along the fault lines of gender and culture, the truth is that the two Englishes that Tan cherished are not valued equally in this society. Despite the creative use of imaginative metaphors in her English, as Tan humorously presented, her mother would never score high in a standard English test that insists on one correct way of linguistic construction. It is no secret that in much of our social discourse and communication practice, the myth persists that what counts as the "normal" standards and criteria for comparing and discussing cultural difference is still the mainstream Eurocentric mode of thinking and doing. In her writing about Asian American women's experience of racism, Shah (1994) said, "For me, the experience of 'otherness,' the formative discrimination in my life, has resulted from culturally different people thinking they were culturally central; thinking that *my* house smelled funny, that *my* mother talked weird, that *my* habits were strange. They were normal; I wasn't." Similarly, in a discussion of the difficult dialogues between black and white women, Houston (1994) points out that when a white woman says "We're all alike," she usually means "I can see how you, a black woman, are like me, a white woman." She does not mean "I can see how I am like you." In other words, whether explicitly or implicitly, "just people" often means "just white people."

Language and identity are always positioned within a hierarchical power structure in which the Chinese American immigrants' form of life has never been granted a status equal to that of their European counterparts in the history of this country. It is one thing to embrace the philosophical wisdom of "having the best of both worlds" but another to confront the real ongoing struggle between languages and identities that most Chinese Americans experience. Bicultural identity cannot be reduced to two neutral, pristine, and equal linguistic domains that one simply picks and chooses to participate in without personal, relational, social, and political consequences. We need to understand the tension and conflict between generations of Chinese American women within the ideological cultural context of racial and sexual inequality and their ongoing contestation of their positions in it.

Through Tan's storytelling in *The Joy Luck Club*, the meaning of "perfect English" is transformed from the mother's naive American dream to the daughter's awakening bicultural disillusionment, as the daughter June laments: "These kinds of explanations made me feel my mother and I spoke two different languages, which we did. I talked to her in English, she answered back in Chinese," and later, "My mother and I never really understood one another. We translated each other's meanings and I seemed to hear less than what was said, while my mother heard more." The lack of shared languages and cultural logics remains a central theme throughout all the narratives in Tan's book. This absence transcends the simple linguistic dichotomies or cultural misunderstandings; both mothers and daughters are negotiating their relational and social positions and contesting their identities as Chinese American women in the languages that can enhance or undermine their power, legitimacy, and voice.

In a similar vein, in *The Woman Warrior* Kingston describes "abnormal" discourse as constructed and experienced by both parents and children in her family. The children in Kingston's family often spoke in English language which their parents "didn't seem to hear"; "the Chinese can't hear American at all; the language is too soft and Western music unhearable." Exasperated and bemused by their Chinese aunt's behavior, the children told each other that "Chinese people are very weird." Angry at the fact that the Chinese were unable, unwilling, or did not see the need to explain things to the children, Kingston writes, "I thought talking and not talking made the differences between sanity and insanity. Insane people were the ones who couldn't explain themselves." While the Chinese American children were frustrated by the impenetrable wisdom spoken or unspoken in the Chinese language, the parents teased the children about the way they spoke in the "ghost's" language and of the craziness and absurdity of doing things in American ways. Insane and absurd in what language(s) and from what cultural perspective(s)? Who has the authority to tell Kingston that Chinese girls are worthless growing up in a society that is supposed to be more egalitarian and liberating for women? What constitutes "normal" and "abnormal" discourse for Chinese American women? What price do they have to pay for being a full participant in either or both cultural worlds?

One intriguing feature in learning to speak and hear incommensurate languages is the process of adjudicating conflicting voices. In Chinese American families, communication can often be characterized by a lack of a shared universe of discourse or a set of mutually intelligible vocabularies. For Kingston, even attempting to engage in a meaningful dialogue with her parents about her confusions and their conflicts became a problem, as she told us, "I don't know any Chinese I can ask without getting myself scolded or teased." Silent and silenced, Kingston was angry at the sexist trivialization of her intellectual interests and academic accomplishment. She writes, "I've stopped checking 'bilingual' on job applications. I could not understand any of the dialects the interviewer at China Airlines tried on me, and he didn't understand me either." Family language almost became a "burden" as Kingston strived to make sense of what it meant to occupy two linguistic and cultural spaces as a Chinese American woman in a patriarchal system. Could her surrender allude to the disappointment and frustration that Chinese Americans as a group feel within the larger society?

In Tan's novel, when one of the daughters, June, did not comply with her mother's wishes, her mother shouted at her in Chinese: "Only two kinds of daughters. Those who are obedient and those who follow their own mind! Only one kind of daughter can live in this house. Obedient daughter!" The mother's injunction is an enactment of her personal power within the family structure, and in this language and cultural logic, June is powerless even if she could speak "perfect" American English, which would give her positional power in a different situation.

Toward the end of the book when Kingston finally confronted her mother with her long list of feelings of guilt being a Chinese American daughter, the linguistic gap and cultural intranslatability resonated throughout their shouting match. Angry, frustrated, hurt, sad, and disappointed, Kingston realized that the confrontation was futile: "And suddenly I got very confused and lonely because I was at the moment telling her my list, and in the telling, it grew. No higher listener. No listener but myself." Once again, their voices did not intermesh, and neither could enter the cultural logic that was specifically structured within the primary language that they spoke. There was no possibility for Kingston to articulate her silence, nor was there space for displaying her mother's good intentions. The celebration of the multiple languages and polyphonic voices seemed elusive. Two generations of women were ultimately torn apart and yet inextricably bonded by the unspeakable cultural tongue. Each in their own way sounded strange, incoherent, crazy, abnormal, and stubborn to the other.

The end of the story of the swan in *The Joy Luck Club* says, "Now the woman was old. And she had a daughter who grew up speaking only English and swallowing more Coca-Cola than sorrow. For a long time now the woman had wanted to give her daughter the single swan feather and tell her, 'This feather may look worthless, but it comes from afar and carries with it all my good intentions.' And she waited, year after year, for the day she could tell her daughter this in perfect American English." As one of the mothers Lindo lamented, "I wanted my children to have the best combination, American circumstances and Chinese character. How could I know these two things do not mix?."

If indeed Chinese Americans are steeped in two languages and two forms of life, one public and dominant, another private and submerged, what is the symbolic significance of using these languages as constructed from various social positions? For the immigrant parents, educating their American-born children to speak the family language is a way to continue the cultural tradition and to instill ethnic pride. Speaking a private language is also an attempt to mark one's difference from the mainstream culture and to resist racism, hegemony, and the overwhelming power of homogenization in this society. In Tan and Kingston's storytelling, speaking Chinese also becomes simply functional for the older immigrants who do not want to participate or/and are not perceived as full participants in the public language. As a result, they remain outsiders within the system; their use of private language marks the central feature of their identity.

Although for many American-born Chinese, using family language can affirm their cultural ties to their ancestors, Kingston also grew up hearing all the derogatory comments about girls in Chinese, the language of foreign and impossible stories to her ear. While speaking her family dialect gives her a sense of connection and intimacy, the private language also symbolizes the oppression, confusion, frustration, madness, and silence that were associated with her coming of age. Using English to speak and write signifies Kingston's rebellion against the patriarchal tradition; it forced her to take a non-Chinese and non-female position in her family and community. For Chinese American women, speaking English affirms their public identity and gives them a legitimate cultural voice to claim for a space in this society. English gives them a means to assert their independence and a tool to fight against sexism and racism that they encounter. Trinh Minh-ha, in an interview, insisted that identity remains as a political/personal strategy of resistance and survival; "the reflexive question asked . . . is no longer: who am I? but when, where, how am I (so and so)?"

It is important to remember that a discussion of uses of language needs to be understood in a political context. Chinese Americans strive for polyphonic coherence within a society that celebrates conformity and homogeneity despite its rhetoric of diversity and pluralism. To mainstream ears, Chinese languages may sound a cacophony of unfamiliar tones and words; this unintelligibility can be associated with foreignness, exotic cultural others, lack of education, or powerlessness. This perceived absence of a shared language and culture (and therefore of disparate social and national interests) can lead to hostility or discrimination toward Chinese Americans.

Through the use of language we create and maintain our social relationships. We accomplish this goal only if an intersubjective discourse exists so that our words and actions are intelligible to others within the community. In Chinese American bicultural experience, this shared language often cannot be taken for granted. In *The Woman Warrior*, Kingston confronted her mother about telling her that she was ugly all the time, to which her mother replied, "That's what we're supposed to say. That's what Chinese say. We like to say the opposite." Here in the mother's language, "truth" is characterized by the logic of the opposite; this "indirect" approach works only if one knows how to hear the statement within the context of a certain kind of relationship. Saying the opposite is what the mother felt obligated to perform; in fact, it was the only language that she could use in order to demonstrate her affection and care for her daughter. Unfortunately, lacking the cultural insight to reverse the logic of her mother's statement, Kingston felt shamed, outraged, and was in turn accused by her mother of not being able to "tell a joke from real life"; her mother shouts at her, "You're not so smart. Can't even tell real from false." Real from false in what language? Where does the humor of this apparent joke for the mother—and humiliation for the daughter—lie in perfect American English?

In *The Joy Luck Club*, the young women's innocence, ignorance, and apathy toward their mother's language seemed to frighten the mothers. June tried to understand her three aunties at the mah jong table:

> And then it occurs to me. They are frightened. In me, they see their own daughters, just as ignorant, just as unmindful of all the truths and hopes they have brought to America. They see daughters who grow impatient when their mothers talk in Chinese, who think they are stupid when they explain things in fractured English. They see that joy and luck do not mean the same to their daughters, that to these closed American-born minds "joy luck" is not a word, it does not exist. They see daughters who will bear grandchildren born without any connecting hope passed from generation to generation

Failure to translate between languages can cost emotional turmoil; it can also silence someone who depends on the English translation to negotiate or accomplish his/her goals. In one of the stories in *The Joy Luck Club*, the daughter Lena was unable to translate her mother's words to her Caucasian stepfather who did not speak Chinese. Since Lena understood the Chinese words spoken by her mother but not the implications, she made up something in her translation and as a result rewrote her mother's story in that episode. Tan intentionally constructed this scene to illustrate the nature of the mother-daughter relationship. Lena was ignorant of both the story that her mother was hinting at and of the Chinese language that her mother was speaking. Kingston's and Tan's writings are characterized by untold stories written in untranslatable language between the two generations of women. McAlister (1992) argued that by failing to translate between languages and stories, Chinese American daughters can participate in the silencing of their mothers. This position seems incongruous in view of Tan's overall agenda in her storytelling. By having all the women narrate their own stories, Tan treats language not just as a tool to reflect upon the past or to celebrate the present, but as a political means to allow Chinese American women to articulate their silenced lives, their otherwise voiceless positions in this society.

Tan writes *The Joy Luck Club* in a language that demands the reader recognize the distinctness of each character, each story and voice, and each mother-daughter relationship. The women in her creation are not just nameless, faceless, or interchangeable Chinese Americans. The interrelated narratives make sense only if readers can discern the specificities of each woman's story as located within the novel. Therefore, "Tan confronts an Orientalist discourse that depends on the sameness of Chinese difference." By granting subjectivity to each woman, Tan compels each to tell her own story in her own words, thus (re)creating the meanings of her life. The mother-daughter tensions as constructed in their own discourse are fraught with complexities of racial, gender, and class issues, not just the simple binary opposition of Americanness and Chineseness, mothers and daughters.

The ability to tell one's own story, to speak one's mind, is the best antidote to powerlessness. Tan's writing instills agency and visibility in Chinese American women. The silence is broken, and their new voices are constructed in collective storytelling, a language of community, without denying or erasing the different positions such collaboration encounters. In a similar vein, Kingston gave the no name woman in her mother's storytelling a voice and a life, a permanent place in American culture; she immortalized this silent woman through her writing: "My aunt haunts me—her ghost drawn to me because now, after fifty years of neglect, I alone devote pages of paper to her." Both Tan and Kingston allow their female characters to reclaim and recreate their identity. "Storytelling heals past experiences of loss and separation; it is also a medium for rewriting stories of oppression and victimization into parables of self-affirmation and individual empowerment." It is possible to celebrate the present without forgetting the past. In an interview when Kingston was contrasting her own American voice in *Tripmaster Monkey* and her translation of Chinese voices in her previous two books, she said, "When I wrote *The Woman Warrior* and *China Men*, as I look back on it, I was trying to find an American language that would translate the speech of the people who are living their lives with the Chinese language. They carry on their adventures and their emotional life and everything in Chinese. I had to find a way to translate all that into a graceful American language, which is my language." Perhaps the boundary between Kingston's two languages/voices is not so clear; of *Tripmaster Monkey*, [a Chinese poet] she said that "I was writing in the tradition of the past." "And I spent this lifetime working on roots. So what they were saying was that I was their continuity."

Both Kingston's and Tan's writings point to the multiplicity and instability of cultural identity for Chinese American women, oscillating and crisscrossing between different Englishes and Chinese dialects that they speak. Although cultural borderlands can be a useful metaphor for "home" for these individuals, we must realize that this home does not rest in a fixed location, nor is it constructed in any one unified language or perfect American English. Neither of the authors is searching for a definitive

Chinese American voice. Through interweaving their own bicultural tongues and multiple imaginative voices, Kingston and Tan focus on women's experiences in their writings and position their uses of languages as central to our understanding of Chinese American women's bicultural world.

Ultimately we see the transformation of double voice in both *The Woman Warrior* and *The Joy Luck Club*. As Trinh put it nicely", . . . the fact one is always marginalized in one's own language and areas of strength is something that one has to learn to live with." Therefore, fragmentation in one's identity becomes "a way of living with differences without turning them into opposites, nor trying to assimilate them out of insecurity." Chinese American women need to cultivate not simply multiple subjectivities but also the ability to move between different languages and positions. As Trinh suggested, this fluidity is a form of challenge and reconstruction of power relations, and women need to learn to use language as a poetic arena of struggle of possibility for transformation. "Ethnic identity is twin skin to linguistic identity—I am my language." Unless Chinese American women acknowledge and celebrate all the Englishes that they grew up with, they cannot accept the legitimacy of their bicultural identity. When asked if she still felt the same contradictions that the protagonist did in *The Woman Warrior*, Kingston said "No, no. I feel much more integrated . . . It takes decades of struggle. When you are a person who comes from a multicultural background it just means that you have more information coming in from the universe. And it's your task to figure out how it all integrates, figure out its order and its beauty. It's a harder, longer struggle."

THE *SALON* INTERVIEW: AMY TAN

The Spirit Within

"My sister Kwan believes she has yin eyes. She sees those who have died and now dwell in the World of Yin, ghosts who leave the mists just to visit her kitchen on Balboa Street in San Francisco. 'Libby-ah,' she'll say to me. 'Guess who I see yesterday, you guess.' And I don't have to guess that she's talking about someone dead."

So begins Amy Tan's third novel, *The Hundred Secret Senses*. Although it has flown up the best-seller lists in the month since its release, the book is a risky departure for the 43-year-old writer, with its emphasis on spirits, magical time-shifts and other unearthly phenomena.

Tan spoke enthusiastically about her book, but admitted that she feared it would be ridiculed as "Chinese superstition." She sat for an interview on the balcony of her San Francisco home, where she surreptitiously lit up a cigarette.

"I don't smoke in public, it's not a good image, it's not a good role model," she apologized. "Not that I actively set out to be one."

With her tiny Yorkshire terrier, Babbazo, snugly ensconced in her lap, Tan, a brilliant smile often belying the frankness of her words, talked about the burdens of fame, the world of Yin, and her struggles with her own emotional demons.

From *Salon* (12 November 1995). © 1995 by *Salon* magazine.

SALON: Have you felt the need to be a role model ever since the success of your first book, "The Joy Luck Club," in 1989?

AMY TAN: I don't feel the need to be a role model, it's just something that's been thrust upon me. Teachers and a lot of Asian-American organizations, for example, say to me, "We need you to come and speak to us because you're a role model."

Are you comfortable with that?

AMY TAN: No. Placing on writers the responsibility to represent a culture is an onerous burden. Someone who writes fiction is not necessarily writing a depiction of any generalized group, they're writing a very specific story. There's also a danger in balkanizing literature, as if it should be read as sociology, or politics, or that it should answer questions like, "What does *The Hundred Secret Senses* have to teach us about Chinese culture?" As opposed to treating it as literature—as a story, language, memory.

Are you finding more or less of that pressure to be categorized?

AMY TAN: It's lessening in the United States. Other Asian-American writers just shudder when they are compared to me; it really denigrates the uniqueness of their own work. I find it happening less here partly because people are more aware now of the flaws of political correctness—that literature has to do something to educate people. I don't see myself, for example, writing about cultural dichotomies, but about human connections. All of us go through angst and identity crises. And even when you write in a specific context, you still tap into that subtext of emotions that we all feel about love and hope, and mothers and obligations and responsibilities.

Speaking of mothers, do you get a hard time from relatives or close friends who think they see themselves in your books? Any accusations of personal secrets being told or confidences betrayed?

AMY TAN: I did, at one point. One relative felt that the story of my grandmother should not have been revealed. My grandmother was the woman (in *The Kitchen God's Wife*) who had been raped, forced to be a concubine, and finally killed herself. My mother, though, got equally angry at the relative and said, "For so many years, I carried this shame on my back, and my mother suffered, because she couldn't say anything to anybody." And she said, "It's not too late; tell the world, tell the world what happened to her." And I take her mandate to be the one that is in my heart, the one that I should follow.

In "The Hundred Secret Senses," you draw much more on the world of the spirit than in your previous books. Was that a theme that you had always wanted to tackle as a writer, or did more personal experiences compel you to address it?

AMY TAN: It's been a part of my life for at least the past 20 years. I've had a lot of death in my life, of people who have been close to me. So I've long thought about how life is influenced by death, how it influences what you believe in and what you look for. Yes, I think I was pushed in a way to write this book by certain spirits—the yin people—in my life. They've always been there, I wouldn't say to help, but to kick me in the ass to write.

Yin people?

AMY TAN: Yin people is the term Kwan uses, because "ghosts" is politically incorrect. People have such terrible assumptions about ghosts—you know, phantoms that haunt you, that make you scared, that turn the house upside down. Yin people are not in our living presence but are around, and kind of guide you to insights. Like in Las Vegas when the bells go off, telling you you've hit the jackpot. Yin people ring the bells, saying, "Pay attention." And you say, "Oh, I see now." Yet I'm a fairly skeptical person, I'm educated, I'm reasonably sane, and I know that this subject is fodder for ridicule.

Does that worry you?

AMY TAN: To write the book, I had to put that aside. As with any book. I go through the anxiety, "What will people think of me for writing something like this?" But ultimately, I have to write what I have to write about, including the question of life continuing beyond our ordinary senses.

You have a very optimistic way of looking at life and death. But these concerns have also been a cause for deep distress in your life, including bouts with serious depression.

AMY TAN: Some of it is probably biochemical, but I think it's also in my family tree. I mean, my grandmother killed herself; she certainly had depression in her life. And anyone, like my mother, who witnessed her own mother killing herself, is going to be prone to the same disease. My own father died of a brain tumor when I was 14. My brother died of the same disease. I didn't do anything about it for a long time, because, like many people, I worried about altering my psyche with drugs. As a writer, I was especially concerned with that. A lot of writers believe that the trauma and the angst that you feel is an essential part of the craft.

And depression is still not respectable—especially taking medication for it.

AMY TAN: People look at me as this very, I don't know, Confucius-like wise person—which I'm not. They don't see all the shit that I've been through (laughs). And going back to the question of being a role model, well, my life hasn't been perfect. I needed help.

What do you take?

AMY TAN: Zoloft. I don't think it's made me a Pollyanna. I can still get angry and upset, but I don't fall into the abyss. I'm grateful that I have some traction now. It doesn't change essentially who you are, but it fixes things just the way insulin does for people with diabetes.

In "The Hundred Secret Senses," the central character, Kwan, is packed off to a California mental hospital for seeing "ghosts." She is somewhat weird, often embarrassing, and doesn't exactly look like Joan Chen. Where did Kwan come from?

AMY TAN: Kwan comes strictly from my imagination, from that world of yin that I write about. I don't know anybody in my life like Kwan, although I feel Kwan-like characters all round me. I would find myself laughing and wondering where these ideas came from. You can call it imagination, I suppose. But I was grateful for wherever they came from.

Olivia, Kwan's American half-sister, is not so happy-go-lucky. Pained, needy, she accidentally pulls heads off pet turtles and has a hard time with other people.

AMY TAN: I took my own skepticism and embedded it into Olivia. Some of her—or the questions that trouble her—are drawn from friends who have the usual existential questions about life and relationships and work and success, and "Why are we here?" and "Why are we with this person?" I've already had interviewers wondering if Olivia's relationship with her husband, Simon, is like my marriage, and I think, "Wait a minute, that's not my husband, that's not my relationship." Certainly all of us have gone through fights with partners in our life, but that's not drawn from my relationships per se. But I know that I'm going to be subject to that assumption.

You write that Olivia's mother suffers "from a kind heart compounded by seasonal rashes of volunteerism." She thinks of her step-daughter Kwan "as a foreign exchange student she would host for a year." In other words, she's a somewhat self-centered ditz—like some of your other less-than-appealing Caucasian characters, in "The Joy Luck Club," for example. Is there a problem between you and white characters?

AMY TAN: (Laughs). No. Some of these characters have to be foils. I needed a mother who was kind of undependable, so that Kwan could become that fount of love that Olivia is looking for. There was no intention—unless there is something subconscious—in trying to depict a Caucasian mother as not so great. I'd have to go through psychotherapy to explore that one. No, some of my best friends are Caucasian.

WENDY HO

Swan-Feather Mothers and Coca-Cola Daughters: Teaching *Amy Tan's* The Joy Luck Club

A. Analysis of Themes and Forms

Amy Tan's *The Joy Luck Club* is not a book in praise of "Oriental exotics" or passive victims. Nonetheless a number of critics and readers think that Amy Tan writes stories about a tantalizing, mysterious, and romanticized Old China or an exoticized Other. Some reviewers comment more about Tan than about the book, referring to her as "the flavor of the month, the hot young thing, the exotic new voice"; others invoke stereotypes in their review of the book: "Snappy as a fortune cookie and much more nutritious, *The Joy Luck Club* is a jolly treatment of familiar conflicts." Another critic asserts that the Joy Luck mothers' memories of China are not anchored in "actual memory," but overtaken by "revery" for the China of their childhood past. He disappoints in encouraging readers to "dream" through the Old China sequences in Tan's book. In *The Big Aiiieeeee!*, a groundbreaking anthology of Asian American literature, the writer-editors are highly critical of what they perceive as Tan's exoticization of China and the Chinese for a white mainstream audience. For them, her book simply resurrects racist images of an inscrutably corrupt East; of heartless, sexist (if not invisible) Chinese men; and of fragile, lotus-blossom women who appear to be too good for the decadent, ignorant society and culture from which they come (Chan et al.). Such one-dimensional Western representations are indeed destructive to the

From *Teaching American Ethnic Literatures; Nineteen Essays*, ed. John R. Maitino and David R. Peck. © 1996 by the University of New Mexico Press.

Asian American community. They are derived from the Orientalist school that Edward Said has so eloquently critiqued in his two books *Orientalism* and *Culture and Imperialism*.

But contrary to what the above critics may say or think, Amy Tan is not out to resurrect shallow stereotypes or Chinese exotica in *The Joy Luck Club*. As teachers, we need to seek out new and empowering interpretive strategies for reading Tan's texts rather than appropriating to ourselves—consciously or unconsciously—ways of reading our emerging writers that are based on racist, sexist perspectives. In this regard, I think it is important for readers to do the hard work of carefully processing the new literary, talk-story texts as intimately anchored not only in the psychodynamic tensions between Chinese immigrant mothers and their Americanized daughters within different familial situations, but also in the concrete socioeconomic, cultural, and historical realities of a hybrid diaspora culture in the United States.

The Joy Luck mothers' imaginations are not so overtaken by "revery" that they cannot comprehend the intersecting struggles of their lives in China or America, or the sexism and racism that they and their families must deal with in their lives. Tan resurrects women's untold personal stories of daily survival and resistance as a form of countermemory: Their multiple stories counter, rather than support, the monolithic imperialist, patriarchal gaze and narratives that have denied them agency, complexity, and visibility in not only their own ethnic communities but also in the dominant Western culture in the U.S. Through her semiautobiographical fiction, Amy Tan advocates the value of reclaiming and understanding these Chinese women's neglected stories in China and America and of preserving and reimagining their Chinese heritage even as they tell of their bewildering new dilemmas as Chinese women in the United States. (For the semiautobiographical nature of her book, consult personal interviews by Seaman; Somogyi and Stanton; Tan, 1990.) Her book is dedicated to her mother, Daisy Tan: "To my mother and the memory of her mother. You asked me once what I would remember. This and much more." From these mother roots, daughter-writers such as Tan draw strength to survive, adapt, and create new stories and myths, new definitions of self-in-community, new strategies for cultural/historical survival that will honor their mothers and communities as well as their Chinese pasts. (See Friedman on the importance of group identity in the discussion of self in the writings of women, minorities, and many non-Western peoples.) Such links of the self in new and old communities will sustain them in the dangerous mine fields of Anglo American life and culture.

Tan's *The Joy Luck Club* is structured around four central mirroring pairs of mothers and daughters: Suyuan Woo and Jing-mei "June" Woo; An-mei Hsu and Rose Hsu Jordan; Lindo Jong and Waverly Jong; and Ying-ying

St. Clair and Lena St. Clair. In *The Joy Luck Club*, the stories of these four pairs are interwoven in four major segments, with the mothers and daughters telling their stories of how it is they came to be where they are in life. Each of the four major segments of the book opens up with a vignette, which is followed by four chapters. The first and last segments involve the Joy Luck mothers' individual stories ("Feathers from a Thousand Li" and "Queen Mother of the Western Skies"). These two mother segments figuratively embrace the two middle segments ("The Twenty-Six Malignant Gates" and "American Translation") in which their daughters speak as second-generation Chinese women in America. In an interesting twist, Jing-mei, the daughter who has reluctantly assumed the place of her deceased mother Suyuan at the mah jong table at the beginning of the book, tells her mother's story in the final chapter, "A Pair of Tickets." She fulfills her mother's dream of returning to China to see her twin daughters—Jing-mei's lost sisters. She finally begins the process of re-identifying with a mother whom she had long neglected—whom she had often dismissed as an exotic Other: The daughter's recognition and reclamation of the intimate bonds with her mother is in counterpoint to the cultural and institutional images and definitions of women as mirrored in patriarchal/imperialist discourse. There is an impending change of guard at the end of the book which suggests the potential for continuity and transformation of mother-and-daughter bonding among a new generation of Chinese American women.

Tan's multiple pairings of mother-daughter stories mirror the strong links between the individual mothers and daughters as well as among all the women of the Joy Luck Club. Rather than focusing on a single primary mother-daughter relationship, Tan gives the reader a sense of the diversity of mother-daughter bonds within Chinese American families. As Tan says, "And when you talk to 100 different people to get their stories on a situation, that's what the truth is. So it's really a multiple story." The links between these mothers and daughters in America are further complicated by the bonds between the Joy Luck mothers and their mothers (and foremothers) in China. Tan enriches the reader's understanding of a single woman's history and of these Chinese American mother-daughter pairs by extending the resonances to the past and to the spidery links to mother-daughter bonds embedded in Chinese culture and society. For example, we witness Lindo Jong's sad separation from her beloved mother and the development of her feisty and clever private self in an arranged marriage—a self that is reflected in a complicated relationship with her own strong-willed daughter. In An-mei Hsu's story, we explore the roots of her frustrations and anger as a woman in the telling of her mother's oppressive life and death as a concubine in feudal China. We begin to understand the links between her personal liberation and the revolutionary changes in China—of a woman and a nation finding a new voice. Tan links Hsu's personal-political struggles with a sociohistorical awareness and participation in her people's struggle for justice and equality. Through the book's intersecting storylines, the reader is exposed to the rich variations and interconnections in the relationships and communications between Chinese mothers and daughters in China and/or in America as they attempt to talk out the silences and distances and to process what is really being described and felt by each other as women.

In *The Joy Luck Club*, the mothers and daughters continually struggle not only to reclaim and speak their stories, but also to "talk back" as complex subjects. But in order to speak up in the larger community and to transform women's lives in a sexist, racist society, Tan's mothers and daughters have to learn to be friends and allies to each other. For women, one important place to begin this primary, necessary work is in the problematic relationships and communications between mothers and daughters. (For an introduction to mother-daughter writing, see, for example, Hirsch.) In *The Joy Luck Club*, mothers and daughters find a compelling need to set the record straight on the specific actualities of their lives in China and America; but they find it difficult to articulate their honest intentions, emotions, and experiences to each other. Jing-mei Woo's mother gives her an heirloom jade pendant—her life's importance—by which she will know her mother's meaning. But as Jing-mei notes, it seemed that she and other jade-pendant wearers were "all sworn to the same secret covenant, so secret we don't even know what we belong to." Much miscommunication takes place between the mothers and daughters. It is a tricky and risky task for them to dredge up and decipher each other's personal stories—these palimpsests that are shrouded in layers of silence, secrecy, pain, ambiguity, collusion, and prohibition within the varied discourses, institutions, and power relations in a society.

However, this is precisely the work that Tan takes up. Each woman has her story of hopes and ambitions, of failure, of survival and resistance. The mothers, for example, must confront the personal archive of tragedy, alienation, suffering, and loss in their own lives; they must negotiate the shame and guilt of leaving country, family, home, and mother. Each woman must wrestle with what to tell the other amid the false images and narratives that obscure or silence their personal stories as Chinese American women. They must overcome the sense that their daughters often look upon them as outcasts, as Other, in America. Jing-mei thinks of her mother's mah jong gatherings as "a shameful Chinese custom, like the secret gathering of the Ku Klux Klan or the tom-tom dances of TV Indians preparing for war." In this less than hospitable context, Suyuan Woo struggles continually to translate her tragic war stories to a resisting daughter. Tan does not neglect to portray the serious dilemmas and ironies that these mothers confront in creating and maintaining a protective environment, a material, cultural and psycho-political bastion, for themselves or their families in America.

Nevertheless, the Joy Luck mothers work painfully to decipher and speak the buried, bittersweet pain of their lives in order to reclaim their own stories and to protect their bewildered daughters from similar pain and oppression as women in America. Through their personal recall, they begin to recognize the insidious links between their pasts and present struggles in America and between their pasts and their daughters' present lives. It is important to read these women's stories as the complicated physical, psychological, cultural, and sociohistorical positionings for personal and communal survival and resistance in the Chinese diaspora communities of the United States. In this light, these stories record not detached reveries or myths about China but, rather, daily heroic actions of many of the Joy Luck mothers, who struggle to raise children under stressful political and sociohistorical conditions.

Like their mothers, daughters must overcome their personal anger, resentment, guilt, and fear toward their mothers. Tan demonstrates how the daughters tend to stereotype their mothers—to freeze them in time as old-fashioned ladies; they do not often give their mothers the space to particularize themselves or to cross over into their lives. They are second-generation, English-speaking Chinese American women, who are located or positioned in an Anglo American homeland that has a long history of oppressing Asian Americans. In living in America, the daughters assimilate certain stereotypical and racist views of the Chinese that alienate them from their own mothers and heritage. They find it distasteful to be identified with their mothers or their stories; with speaking the Chinese language, or with keeping the old ways and customs. Joy Luck daughters often fail to recognize the difficult but vital work and nurture of their working-class, immigrant Chinese mothers. Yuppie Waverly Jong, for example, makes up jokes to tell her friends about her mother's arrival in America and about her parents meeting and marriage. She trivializes their stories of struggle and joy. Waverly does not know the true story about the difficulties of her feisty immigrant mother; the poignant story of how her parents courted by surmounting ethnic and linguistic difficulties; or the story of how her name was chosen to express her mother's love and hopes for her.

Within this problematic framework, the Joy Luck women struggle to maintain vital communication with each other and to piece together the fragmented memories and talk-story of their actual lives. In *The Joy Luck Club*, it is a struggle, with varying successes and failures, for the mother-daughter pairs to know and love each other for their own strengths, weaknesses, and contexts. As we see in the individual stories, it is easy for mothers and daughters to get lost in the intense psychodynamic love-hate struggles within themselves and with each other. Both can be nurturing and suffocating, protective and negligent, trusting and distrustful, arrogant and humble, powerful and weak, affiliative and competitive toward each other. Each Joy Luck mother-daughter pair attempts to articulate positions that are rooted in their intertwined needs for individuation, mutual respect, and attachment to each other and their communities.

In addition, these psychodynamic tensions are embedded in particular socioeconomic and historical circumstances in China and in America that further complicate their relationship and communications with each other; that is, internal tensions between mothers and daughters are exacerbated and even generated by external factors. In *The Joy Luck Club*, mothers and daughters often have a difficult time smoothly negotiating the great sociohistorical expanses of their specific *weltanschaung*. For example, mothers and daughters are separated by historical time, cataclysmic natural disasters and wars, generations, classes, sociocultural systems and values, and languages. The traumatic translation of devalued and ambitious Chinese-speaking immigrant mothers from their motherland to an unfriendly and alien country and the assimilation of their second-generation, English-speaking Chinese daughters into mainstream America cause serious fractures in their relationship and communication with each other.

For the Joy Luck women to communicate with each other and to speak up as women against the invisibility—the distorted images and stereotypes of women in China and America—is to begin to imagine the histories that have been left out. As some of their own mothers struggled to teach them, Joy Luck mothers want to teach their daughters how to acknowledge and deal with pain; how to know true friends; how to trust that their mothers know them inside and out; how to be free of confusion; how to survive under tricky and marginal circumstances with grace and joy luck. Some of the mothers especially desire to pass on to their daughters a sense of *shou*, a respect and honor for their mothers; *nengkan*, an ability to accomplish anything they put their mind to; and *chuming*, an inner knowing of each other as women. Most desire to reclaim their daughters by fighting for their hearts and minds and by responsibly educating them to survive and to subvert the oppressive systems in which they live. Joy Luck mothers teach their daughters that personal and cultural identity need to be maintained not only through the preservation of Chinese heritage but also through a continually active, fluid, multidimensional agency that can negotiate the fluctuations of oppressive social, cultural, and historical processes.

On the one hand, Asian American women have suffered under imperialist and patriarchal power structures. To deny these oppressive factors in any culture—whether in China or America—is, as Frank Chin likes to say, to live in the "fake world," not the "real world." The Asian American mothers and daughters in *The Joy Luck Club* are struggling subjects and agents encountering a not very perfect world in China and in America. Sometimes they lose their battles in the oppressive systems in which they live and position themselves; they comply, negotiate, and/or betray themselves and others in their search for sheer survival or status within systems of power. Tan shows us the complicity and compromise that can mire her female characters as they struggle to come to consciousness and voice about their lives and circumstances. For example, women are complicit in destroying An-mei's mother through the patriarchal power arrangements of family and society. Wu Tsing's childless Second Wife arranges to entrap An-mei's mother as a concubine for her husband. As a rich woman, Second Wife uses the borrowed class, wealth, and power of her husband to oppress and manipulate other women. This oppression of the other wives is her attempt to guarantee her own tenuous position and status in Wu Tsing's competitive female household. Tan is not out to valorize or privilege all women's language and actions. She paints a painfully problematic picture of women's complicity not only in another woman's oppression, but in their own continuing oppression in and maintenance of male-dominated culture.

On the other hand, Asian women are not always or simply powerless, passive, exploited dupes and sexual objects, domestic drudges, illiterates, and/or traditional women in patriarchal or imperialist systems. In teaching this book, one must not neglect to take into account that Tan shows us how ordinary women, located in the specific context of their own times and personal circumstances, have challenged and subverted the socioeconomic and political systems under which they have lived and are living in many different ways. At the same time that their lives bespeak oppression and tragedy, the Joy Luck mothers do not neglect to pass on empowering interventions to their daughters. These resistances counter the patriarchal and imperialist systems that they are exposed to in China and America, which have forced them to speak, see, think, and act often in disempowering terms.

Such communication provides vital entry into the past, present, and future. The mothers' life-stories are the valuable maps not only of the powerlessness, servility, frustration, defeat, and compromise, but also of the powerful strategies of intervention and subversion that help women survive with a certain amount of grace, anger, strength, connectedness, and love. Mothers and daughters come to realize their fierce love and respect for each other as friends and survivors. They come to realize that there are rich challenges and meanings embodied even in the silences, fragments, tensions, and differences.

Doing the work of talk-story as a way to resist oppressive, monolithic patriarchal and imperialist institutions and metanarratives can lead to the inscription of new and fluid woman-centered spaces for women. In *The Joy Luck Club*, we learn just how vital it is for mothers and daughters to continually talk-story—not to wait, for instance, to speak only until spoken to or given authority to do so or till one can speak perfect American English. It can be personally and politically empowering and heroic for women to tell their stories and attend to each other—not to be decentered objects whose stories are continually co-opted or translated for them or to them by those in power. In this way, women can be empowered to challenge society. During the Chinese Revolution, Chinese women learned to stand up and speak against not only their landlords but also their husbands and fathers. The slogan for this emancipation of people was *fanshen*, which meant "to stand up and overturn the oppressing classes." Women learned to speak the bitterness in their daily lives. Within their consciousness-raising women's groups in the countryside and cities, women learned, first of all, to speak up about the poverty, the hunger, the physical and psychological abuse and fear, the socioeconomic and political inequities. Women had access to each other's true feelings and contexts in an affiliative, nurturing environment. In this way, they learned they were not alone, separate from other women or other oppressed groups. Many Chinese women were empowered to speak and act together in transforming their lives and society. Likewise, Tan's mothers want to teach their daughters how to read situations clearly and how to stand up and fight for themselves. They want their daughters to be bolder, more self-assured women; to be independent from their husbands; to have status and voice on their own merit. As the critic bell hooks has powerfully stated, talking back is a way of speaking up for oneself as a woman, boldly and defiantly. It is "not solely an expression of creative power; it is an act of resistance, a political gesture that challenges politics of domination that would render us nameless and voiceless. As such it is a courageous act—as such, it represents a threat. To those who wield oppressive power, that which is threatening must necessarily be wiped out, annihilated, silenced."

Like Maxine Hong Kingston, Amy Tan is a daughter-writer, who has come to realize that locating, defining, and reporting women's stories and the crimes against women and community are part of the constructive, articulated anger and revenge against the narratives and institutions that oppress them. To recover multiple histories and to talk back as women united is to do real battle against oppression in their personal and communal lives. In reading Tan, one becomes acutely aware that this is serious, painful, complicated excavatory work; it is also subversive, creative, freeing, and responsible work for mothers and daughters who wish to connect as women-allies.

B. Teaching *The Joy Luck Club*

An understanding of the Joy Luck mothers' (and their foremothers') Chinese past can help make the problematic interactions with their second-generation Americanized daughters—how they perceive and treat them and why—more accessible to readers. Teachers can assign introductory background readings on women in Chinese and Chinese American history. The mother-and-daughter relationships cannot be fully understood as simply personal, internal problems to be worked out between Chinese mothers and their daughters. The bonds are problematized or complicated, in part, by their embeddedness in the particular psychological, socioeconomic, cultural, and historical realities of a traditional Confucian society that socialized and oppressed women in China.

As Julia Kristeva notes, Confucianists saw women as small human beings (*hsiao ren*) to be categorized with babies and slaves. Women were not suited by nature for the intellectual life of a scholar or a statesman. Women's lives were to revolve around the Three Obediences and Four Virtues:

> The Three Obediences enjoined a woman to obey her father before marriage, her husband after marriage, and her eldest son after her husband's death. The Four Virtues decreed that she be chaste; her conversation courteous and not gossipy; her deportment graceful but not extravagant; her leisure spent in perfecting needlework and tapestry for beautifying the home.

These delimiting societal prescriptions for women's gender roles and for a "true" Chinese womanhood can permit the physical and psychological abuse of women. The Joy Luck mothers experience their mothers' as well as their own difficult compromises and failures in a restrictive patriarchal culture and society. For example, An-mei Hsu learns the lessons that attempt to strain and destroy her relationship with her mother. Both An-mei and her mother live in traditional familial and societal structures, which often deny their personal needs, sufferings, and struggles and ask them to conform to a male-dominated culture against their own individual and common interests as women. An-mei grows up with stories, which attempt to break the spirit of strong-willed girls, the disobedient types—like her hidden self. These patriarchal stories are powerful forms of socialization into her proper and public roles in traditional Chinese society as a daughter, wife, mother, woman. The film version of Tan's *The Joy Luck Club* (Wayne Wang) dramatically depicts the tragic experiences of the mothers in China and its parallels and consequences in the lives of their daughters in the United States. A viewing of the film—a real tearjerker—could provide another way to access the psychodynamic tensions between the mother-daughter pairs in the book. For a view of women's lives in prerevolutionary China, students can read the Chinese novel *The Family* by Pa Chin. The film *Small Happiness* (Carma Hinton and Richard Gordon) can provide a sense of women's lives in a specific Chinese context. In exploring the impact of a Chinese Confucian system on women's socialization into gender roles and identity, students can better understand the relationships of the Joy Luck mothers to their own mothers in China. In addition, this information can help students to understand the complex interactions between the Joy Luck mothers and their own daughters in America.

The historical events and natural disasters in China also play a role in shaping the Joy Luck mothers. They and their mothers before them, in one way or another, experience a range of horrific wars and chaos, evacuations, deaths, economic turmoil, revolutionary changes, poverty, floods, and famines that seriously impinge on their personal relationships and communications with their daughters. In the 1800s to middle 1900s, there were horrendous wars for colonial dominance over China waged by imperialist powers such as England, the United States, and Japan. There was bloody civil war between the Chinese Communist Party (Mao Zedong) and the Guomindang (Chiang Kai-shek) rumbling through China. Chinese women suffered the terrible consequences of these chaotic events, especially the toll they took on the socioeconomic and political situations in their daily lives. For instance, Suyuan Woo's life, fears, and ambitions are clearly influenced by the chaos and brutalities of war, separation from family, death of a husband, and loss of her baby daughters. Suyuan's abandonment of her twin daughters during her escape from the invading Japanese is vividly portrayed the film version of *The Joy Luck Club*. Young Lindo Jong remembers the painful, lonely separation from her beloved mother: she is sent to her boy-husband's household after disastrous floods, famine, and poverty make it difficult for the family to keep a "useless" daughter. Ying-ying St. Clair's concerns for her daughter's safety and her own fears at being sexually harassed on an Oakland street by a stranger could be rooted in her own bitter experiences as a lone married woman migrating from the poor countryside to Shanghai, a city notorious for its foreign decadence and the murder, rape, kidnapping, and prostitution of Chinese women in the early to middle 1900s. However, it was also a significant revolutionary period of change, not only in terms of women's rights but also for the Chinese nation. Students need to keep in mind that the Joy Luck mothers are the products of these revolutionary times. They are women of old and new China.

Besides an understanding of the Joy Luck mothers' Chinese roots, it is important to consider their traumatic translation to the United States. The mothers are excited by the potential opportunities in America for themselves and their families. But they are also socialized into silence by American racism and haunted by the history of immigration policies that have excluded Asians from entry into America. Before the arrival of the Joy Luck mothers in 1949, America already had a long and ugly record of discriminatory attitudes and policies aimed not only against successive groups of Asians, but also specifically against the Chinese. Besides numerous Chinese immigration exclusionary laws enacted between 1882 and 1904, there were also a number of immigration policies that specifically deterred the immigration of Chinese women to America (such as the 1875 Page Law and the 1924 Immigration Act). These restrictive forms of social and legal legislation affected the numbers of Asian women entering the country and the subsequent formation of Asian families in America. Racist/sexist stereotypes portrayed Chinese women as lewd and immoral women, who were unfit to enter the country. Sensational newsmedia coverage on the evils of Chinese prostitution created the long-standing stereotype of Chinese women as prostitutes. As audiovisual resources, films such as *Slaying the Dragon* (Deborah Gee) and *New Year* (Valerie Soe) can provide a visual introduction to the many stereotypes of Asian American women/people. With this long history of racism and sexism in the United States, Tan shows us why it is not difficult to understand the Chinese immigrant mothers' fear of the police, deportation, and backlash from white Americans based on their race and gender.

Despite all her years in America, An-mei Hsu lives with fears of deportation. An-mei's fears are well grounded, especially if one remembers America's severe anti-communist paranoia of the 1950s. Likewise, Ying-ying St. Clair is forced to invent a fictive self that is oriented to her present and future life in America, but which does not account for her frightening past life. In this foreign and suffocating space, she feels numb, off balance, and lost, living in small houses, doing servant's work, wearing American clothes, learning Western ways and English, accepting American ways without care or comment, and raising a distant daughter. Upon her arrival in America, Ying-ying is processed at Angel Island Immigration Station, where agents try to figure out her classification: war bride, displaced person, student, or wife. She is renamed Betty St. Clair; she loses her Chinese name and identity as

Gu Ying-ying and gains a new birthdate. In the Chinese lunar calendar, she is no longer a tiger but a dragon. It takes her a long time to recover and pass on her tiger spirit to her daughter Lena.

In contrast to the mothers, the daughters, born and raised in contemporary America, have assimilated more easily into the dominant society. But Tan portrays the great cost of assimilation in the miscommunications between the Joy Luck mothers and daughters. Under such circumstances, how can mothers tell their stories to their insider/outsider daughters? How can the Joy Luck mothers articulate their stories fully if they feel they must hide or deny their past? their language in America? How can Americanized Chinese daughters begin to understand the fractured narratives that surface, made up, as they are, of so many lies and truths, so many protective layers set up against the outsiders' *chuming*, an inner knowing, of them? What are the advantages and disadvantages of assimilation for these mothers and daughters? How can these women learn to be friends and allies to each other? How are language and strategies for survival and resistance passed from mothers to daughters? She demonstrates how many intertwined dilemmas can impede or frustrate clear access by daughters to their mothers and to the full stories of their mother's and family's life and history in China and America. Nevertheless, Tan's text emphasizes that this difficult work of recovery is vital to women's well-being and solidarity with each other.

Another way of accessing Tan's book is to analyze her use of traditional Chinese legends (for example, the Moon Lady story) and images to articulate the concerns of Chinese American women. For instance, the Joy Luck mothers want their daughters to turn into beautiful swans—perfect, happy, successful, and independent women. In traditional Chinese stories, swans symbolize married, heterosexual love. Tan subverts and re-interprets the traditional image of swans by applying it to the silenced and intimate pairings between women. In this case, a mother and her daughter. The traditional symbols and narratives are being appropriate, reconstructed, or ruptured by writers like Tan (and Maxine Hong Kingston) who do not wish to focus on the master narratives of patriarchy, but to focus instead on the powerful stories of love and struggle between mothers and daughters, between women in China and in America. The stories in *The Joy Luck Club* give voice to the desires and experiences of female characters who have not had the advantage to write or tell their stories as men have had. It is their neglected stories that they tell and attempt to transmit to their daughters in the oral traditions of talk-story. These hybrid talk-story narratives challenge those who would deny or lessen the power, beauty, value, and pain in these women's lives. This is what Maxine Hong Kingston spent a lot of time learning in her memoir

The Woman Warrior: "The reporting is the vengeance—not the beheading, not the gutting, but the words." The personal stories of the Joy Luck mothers do battle through gossip, circular talking, cryptic messages/caveats, dream images, bilingual language, and talk-story traditions—not in the linear, logical, or publicly authorized discourse in patriarchal or imperialist narratives. This is talk that challenges the denial of Asian American women's voices and identities—denials not only by a male-dominated Chinese society and a Eurocentric American society but also by their very own daughters who have become so Americanized that they can barely talk-story with their mothers. In many ways, Tan's book can be fruitfully compared with *The Woman Warrior*. As heroic paper daughters in quest of their mothers' stories, Tan and Kingston empower not only their mothers but also themselves and their racial/ethnic communities through a psychic and oral/literary birthing that keeps alive the intimate, ever-changing record of tragedies, resistances, and joy luck for all people.

In the following section, I have included a number of additional discussion and paper topic questions that would be useful in teaching Tan's *The Joy Luck Club*.

1. What are the experiences most remembered by the mothers? Where is "home" for them? How do the experiences of the mothers resonate in the lives of their daughters? Can one see parallels in the daughters' lives? What expectations do individual mothers have for their daughters? and vice versa? What are the obstacles—social, economic, psychological, cultural, historical—that impact on the communications between the mothers and daughters? How does assimilation into dominant Anglo American culture affect their relationship? Is it important for daughters and mothers to communicate with each other? Why? How do mothers and daughters specifically find ways to survive and resist their multiple oppressions as Chinese American women?

2. Discuss how Tan portrays the acquisition of gender identity and roles in the early childhood of the Joy Luck mothers in stories such as "The Moon Lady," "The Scar," or "The Red Candle." How does Tan convey through the language and images the particular conflicts and tensions within the different women? Do they simply adjust to the repression of their own private desires and dreams? How do they negotiate or resist patriarchal/imperialist oppression? Do they succeed and/or fail in their attempts?

3. Discuss the style or structure of Tan's text—for example, her use of a first-person point of view in the text. Or why and how does Tan use and/or transform the Chinese talk-story tradition or the images and legends in her own Chinese American stories? In regard to these topics, students could expand the discussion by comparing and contrasting two other Chinese

American mother-daughter literary texts—Jade Snow Wong's *Fifth Chinese Daughter* (1945) and Maxine Hong Kingston's *The Woman Warrior* (1977).

4. (a) For a broader analysis of Asian American mother-daughter interactions, compare/contrast *The Joy Luck Club* with Tan's second novel *The Kitchen God's Wife*, which focuses on the difficult relationship and revelations between the immigrant mother Jiang Weili and her Chinese American daughter Pearl. *The Joy Luck Club* can also be used with Faye Myenne Ng's first novel *Bone*, which reveals the trauma and grief of a San Francisco Chinatown family attempting to deal with the suicide of one of their three daughters. Tan's book also works well with Joy Kogawa's *Obasan* or Hisaye Yamamoto's *Seventeen Syllables and Other Stories*. Both writers deal with the multiple tensions between immigrant mothers and their second-generation daughters in the Japanese American community before, during, and after World War II. There are also a good selection of essays, short stories, and poems by other Asian American writers on this topic in Asian American anthologies.

(b) Other mother-daughter writings that can be used with Tan's book include Kim Chernin's *In My Mother's House: A Daughter's Story*, Edwidge Danticat's *Breath, Eyes, Memory*, Audre Lorde's *Zami: A New Spelling of My Name*, and Paule Marshall's *Brown Girl, Brownstones*. For example, Paule Marshall's novel, set in Brooklyn during the period of the Depression and World War II, depicts the struggles of a Barbadian immigrant family as it confronts poverty and racism in the United States. In the story, Selina Boyce, a young daughter searching for identity, must confront and resolve the contradictory feelings she has toward her hardworking, ambitious mother. Possible questions to help promote discussion around these novels include the following: What personal, cultural, and sociohistorical struggles do women encounter in their families and mixed cultures in the United States? In what ways do they attempt to construct multiple selves, subjectivities, or positionings that have value against the meaninglessness, oppression, and violence (psychic and physical) that they encounter in their lives? Do they succeed and/or fail in their attempts? How do women empower or destroy other women? How do these diverse writers find innovative ways to rupture racist/sexist language and institutions through their creative use of language and/or narrative strategies? Are there similarities and/or differences in their writing strategies/tactics, stories, experiences? What type of identification and valorization of a women's culture is portrayed in the texts?

5. To provide for more inclusive and personal participation in the discussion of the book, students can compare their own relationships with their mothers and families and how they are situated and constructed in specific and diverse racial/ethnic, social, cultural, and historical contexts.

This can be done in small group discussions, journal entries, and/or an oral history project.

6. (a) Students might wish to see the film version of *The Joy Luck Club* and discuss how the film might significantly differ from the book. What stories were left out? which ones kept? and why? Were there any modifications in the stories portrayed in the film? Why? How are men depicted in the book and film? Are the issues of racism and sexism in the United States discussed or left invisible in the film? Why and/or why not?

(b) Compare/contrast the portrayals of the mother-daughter relationship in *The Joy Luck Club* with another film directed by Wayne Wang, entitled *Dim Sum*, which also portrays the daily interactions between an immigrant Chinese mother and her daughter. What are the similarities and/or differences in the representations of Chinese Americans and their experiences in these two films? What were the production contexts (such as funding, decision-making process, studio, writing, and directing) for these two films by Wayne Wang? How do these institutional contexts impact on the final aesthetic product that is produced? Who are the audiences for these two films?

E. D. HUNTLEY

The Hundred Secret Senses

Having explored the dynamics of the mother-daughter relationship in her first two novels, Amy Tan turns to the sisterly bond in her third, *The Hundred Secret Senses*, published in 1995. Reviews for the new novel were mixed; some commentators described it as Tan's best work while others found fault with either Tan's focus on supernatural elements or with the novel's conclusion. Most reviewers did, however, acknowledge Tan's gift for storytelling, and many pointed out that Kwan in *Secret Senses* is one of Tan's most original and best character creations.

Readers familiar with Tan's work will immediately recognize in *The Hundred Secret Senses* a number of distinctive Tan trademarks: a strong sense of place, a many-layered narrative, family secrets, generational conflict, Chinese lore and history, and an engrossing story. Employing multiple settings—twentieth-century San Francisco and Changmian, China, as well as nineteenth-century China during the final years of the Taiping Rebellion—Amy Tan spins out *The Hundred Secret Senses* across two centuries and two continents, unraveling the mysteriously interwoven stories of Olivia Bishop and her half sister, Li Kwan, and Nelly Banner and her "loyal friend" Nunumu.

The Hundred Secret Senses is a novel of contrasts—the story of two sisters, two cultures, two lives, two centuries linked by loyalties and betrayals,

From *Amy Tan: A Critical Companion* by E. D. Huntley. © 1998 by E. D. Huntley.

love and loss, life and death. At the heart of the novel is the complex and uneasy relationship between California-born Olivia and her much older Chinese-born half-sister, Kwan, who comes to America when she is eighteen years old. The daughter of Jack Yee and his discarded first wife, Kwan is markedly Chinese, while Olivia, whose mother is Jack Yee's second—and American—wife, is so definitively American that her idea of ethnic food is take-out Chinese cuisine. Perhaps because she is already an adult when she emigrates, Kwan never truly assimilates into American culture, although she takes an unrestrained delight in all things American. Unfortunately, Olivia as a child is frequently mortified by her unusual new sister who asks too many odd questions, never learns to speak fluent English, and engulfs her with loyalty and devotion combined with a goofy determination to maneuver Olivia into sharing all of her secrets.

The most unnerving of those secrets is Kwan's unshakeable belief that she is gifted with *yin eyes*, a term that she employs (and that Amy Tan invented) to explain her frequent conversations with people who are already dead and who inhabit an otherworldly existence that she calls "the World of Yin" (another Tan invention). Disturbed by Kwan's nonchalant communication with ghosts, Olivia nevertheless grows up half-listening, but very much against her will, to Kwan's stories about *yin* people and a previous life in nineteenth-century China. Although Olivia claims not to believe in the *yin* people, she has actually seen (or perhaps dreamed vividly about) at least one *yin* person when she was a child; and she has no compunction about enlisting their aid through Kwan's mediation in her campaign to marry Simon Bishop. As an adult, Olivia tries to distance herself from Kwan and her tales, but Kwan's stories do not disappear with time. In fact, as Kwan approaches her fiftieth birthday, her compulsion to talk about the *yin* people and her life in China increases tremendously, and Olivia finds herself bombarded with more stories and with snippets of reminiscences that Kwan seems to expect her mystified sister to "remember" or at least recognize somehow.

When the Bishop marriage disintegrates after seventeen years, Kwan begins to insist that she and her *yin* friends believe that Olivia and Simon should put behind them their divorce plans and instead work toward reconciliation. Finally, Kwan maneuvers the estranged pair into accompanying her to China to visit the village of her childhood and adolescence. Despite their misgivings about the journey, Olivia and Simon agree to go, and when they arrive in Kwan's home village of Changmian, they are almost instantly catapulted into an alien landscape in which the dominant features are both unrecognizably strange and disturbingly familiar to Olivia. In this disorienting setting, she and Simon are forced to confront the hidden resentments and disguised angers that have destroyed their marriage.

Interwoven with Olivia's story is Kwan's intermittent but compelling series of narratives of her past life as a girl named Nunumu in the nineteenth century during which she claims that she worked as a servant in a household of English missionaries. Central to that life was the close friendship that developed between Nunumu and Miss Banner, whose affair with a bogus American general puts the entire group of foreigners in danger, and whose later love for a half-Chinese–half-American interpreter leads to her death as well as that of the faithful Nunumu.

Kwan's need to reconcile past and present, and her desire to connect her lives, serve as the catalyst for the revelation of secrets, the articulation of unspoken pain, the reaffirmation of love and—at the end—the payment of old debts of loyalty. And although Kwan mysteriously disappears before Olivia's and Simon's daughter is born, the reader is left with the suggestion that the child is Kwan's gift to the couple as well as a reminder of Kwan's place in their history.

PLOT DEVELOPMENT

The plot of *The Hundred Secret Senses* follows two narrative threads: Olivia's search for an integrated self, and Kwan's desire to undo the damage of a century-old mistake. Although the two are closely related, the connections between them do not immediately become obvious but emerge gradually as elements of each plot come to light and reveal echoes of the other.

Borrowing a technique from the classical epic, Amy Tan begins the novel *in medias res*, or—colloquially translated—in the middle of the action. Over a century earlier in China, Kwan—with the very best intentions—told a lie, fabricating a story that had the unforeseen effect of disrupting the lives of two people and abruptly terminating the romance that had begun between them. The plot that has Kwan at its center is the history of her previous existence as Nunumu; the events of her life gradually reveal the incidents that lead inexorably toward the mistake that separates Miss Banner and Yiban. Now in California, Kwan is devoting her energies to the cause of rectifying her mistake and reuniting the lovers. Meanwhile, in the narrative of Olivia's efforts to discover what she wants her life to become, Olivia and Simon already are separated and have initiated the legal transactions that will lead to divorce. Both women tell their stories, but whereas Olivia's narratives suggest interior monologues with a pervasive component of self-questioning and no identifiable audience, Kwan's stories—which are embedded in Olivia's—are clearly addressed to Olivia.

As Olivia sorts through the emotional chaos resulting from her separation from Simon, she repeatedly is reminded of the events of their courtship, the early years of their marriage, and their more recent attempts to revive the companionship they felt when they were younger. Because Simon was and is her first and only love, Olivia is not dealing well with the break-up of her marriage, and Kwan, who is still the protective older sister although they are both adults, worries constantly about Olivia, inviting her to dinner, dropping in for brief visits, offering the opinion that the separation is a mistake and that Olivia and Simon should reconcile. In the first half of the novel, each overture by Kwan prompts Olivia to remember a story that Kwan has told her, and each story told by Kwan in turn somehow returns the narrative to Olivia's emotional dilemma. With each new story, the outlines of connections become clearer. Initially, it appears that Kwan wants to bring the couple back together because she was responsible for the evening during which Elza—a *yin* person and Simon's first love who had been dead for a while—supposedly told Simon to forget her and to find happiness with Olivia. But Kwan's stories and everyday conversation are laced with oblique references to her belief that the rightness of Olivia's and Simon's union was determined by events in the distant past, and eventually Kwan manages to persuade Simon and Olivia to join her on a trip to China where, she points out mysteriously, they will discover the true pattern of their lives.

During the China trip, Olivia's and Kwan's narratives abruptly change. Removed from the familiar and confronted with a new culture, Olivia curtails her litany of past rejections and begins instead to detail events as they happen; and because she is in China, Olivia no longer has to rely on her memory of Kwan's stories—China is all around her to be experienced. Kwan, for her part, increases the number and frequency of her stories about Nunumu and Miss Banner, adding stories that Olivia has never heard—for instance, the story of Yiban and the last days in the Ghost Merchant's house, or the tale of the flight to the mountains. Early in the novel, Kwan's stories emerge as Olivia's memories, but in the final chapters, Kwan tells her stories in the immediate present. Gone is the slow gentle rhythm of memory; each tale now is urgent, immediate, triggered by the sight of a mountain or the taste of a special dish or, ultimately, the very palpable presence of a music box that Kwan claims to have hidden in a cave over a century earlier. Kwan's final stories clarify connections: Olivia and Simon are Miss Banner and Yiban, and Kwan has brought them to Changmian to reunite them. The novel ends with an epilogue narrated by Olivia. She and Simon are working toward reconciliation. More important, they have a daughter who was conceived in China, and who is—Olivia firmly believes—Kwan's final gift to them.

NARRATIVE STRATEGIES

Tan employs the juxtaposition of past and present as a narrative device for her story of the indestructibility of love and loyalty. Past and present are so closely interrelated that Olivia ultimately admits to being occasionally confused about whether an event actually occurred or is merely an episode in one of Kwan's frequently recounted stories. Toward the end of the novel, as Olivia and Kwan turn over the contents of the ancient music box that the latter says she hid in a cave more than a hundred years earlier, Olivia's logical mind races from one explanation to another. Always the rational American woman of the 1990s, Olivia is inclined to doubt what her senses suggest; nevertheless, she cannot dismiss the fact of Kwan's unflinching candor. In their time together, Olivia has never known Kwan to lie; in fact, Kwan says only what she truly believes to be true. And although Olivia knows that she should believe Kwan even now, another question surfaces: "[I]f I believe what she says, does that mean I now believe she has *yin* eyes?" At that moment, Olivia realizes what she has known, has in fact believed all along—since childhood—that Kwan does remember events, the memory of which defies rational explanation.

Events in the past clearly and significantly influence the lives of both Olivia and Kwan. They are sisters, thanks to Jack Yee's two marriages and the shameful act of thievery that provided him with the wherewithal to abandon a wife and child, to discard an identity, and to begin a new life and new family in America. Through her conversations with her *yin* friends about Olivia's marital problems, Kwan bridges the chronological gap between her two lives, and Olivia is forced to endure advice and comments on her marriage from a certain Lao Lu, a friend of Kwan's from the Taiping days in the Ghost Merchant's house. Not even Olivia's marriage is immune to the influence of the past: after nearly two decades of marriage, Simon still appears to be obsessed with his first love who was killed in an avalanche.

During the visit to China, Kwan becomes more and more insistent that she and Olivia have had a previous life together, and when the sisters are together on the mountain, Olivia begins to half believe that she does indeed recognize in her present circumstances a series of strong resonances from another time. Whether these frissons of memory are remnants of Kwan's stories or genuine recollections from Olivia's past is immaterial. What is clear is that Olivia finds the more distinctive elements of the Guilin landscape disturbingly familiar.

Present and past finally collide on a rain-drenched mountain just beyond Changmian. Assailed from all directions by a cascade of sensory and emotional stimuli (Kwan's final story about her last hours in the nineteenth century, a hilly landscape that possesses a dreamlike familiarity combined with jarring strangeness, Simon's disappearance into the cold mist, Kwan's rediscovery of the music box that she last saw when she was Nunumu, and finally Kwan's revelation of the truth about Simon and Elza), Olivia is drawn into an admission that her history with Kwan could have begun near this mountain in an earlier century. It remains only for Olivia to unearth the jars full of duck eggs that Kwan says Nunumu buried during the Taiping troubles. As Olivia holds the ancient crumbling duck eggs in her cupped hands, the act liberates her from the doubts that have undermined all of her relationships. And although Kwan vanishes into the Changmian caves and is never found despite an intensive and protracted search, Olivia believes that the daughter who is born to her and Simon nine months later is a gift from Kwan. The child is not Kwan, exactly, but she is connected with Kwan in some mysterious way—and in that little girl, the past and the present are fused into wholeness and the future.

As she does in her other novels, Tan relies on formal storytelling as a narrative strategy in *The Hundred Secret Senses.* Both Kwan's nineteenth-century existence as Nunumu and her twentieth-century childhood in Changmian before her emigration to America emerge through narrative set pieces that Kwan performs as though they are legends or folktales, artifacts of an oral tradition that she feels impelled to pass on to Olivia who is her captive audience.

Tan uses the flashback technique to superb effect in the novel. New words, chance remarks, familiar objects and mementos, the taste of traditional Chinese dishes, and celebrations trigger Kwan's recollections, prompting her to narrate vignettes, brief tales, events, the particulars of specific episodes in her former lives. In one instance, when she overhears the neighborhood children referring to her as "a retard" and forces Olivia to define the word, Kwan suddenly is reminded of Miss Banner's early attempts to speak Chinese, and she tells Olivia that Nunumu initially thought that Miss Banner's inability to speak or understand Chinese indicated a lack of intelligence. On occasion, Kwan says, Nunumu actually laughed at Miss Banner's feeble attempts to converse in the vernacular. The memory prompts Kwan immediately to launch into an account of Miss Banner's first garbled description of her early life. Because Miss Banner cannot speak adequate Chinese, she ends up thoroughly confusing Nunumu by telling an impossibly surrealistic story about her origins, but Nunumu's patience with her mistress eventually results in her success at teaching Miss Banner how to view the world "exactly as a Chinese person" would.

By providing multiple versions of and varying perspectives on events that are central to the novel, Tan explores the ways through which storytellers create meaning on many levels and from different points of view. In some cases, the plurality of versions is the inadvertent result of misunderstandings, incomplete information, or even partial fabrication; in other cases, variant editions of a story signal the storyteller's intent to deceive. Tan seems to be suggesting that the truth exists both in each version of a story and somewhere in the unspoken narrative or in the spaces between stories.

A hallmark of *The Hundred Secret Senses* is the novel's precarious position somewhere between the real and the surreal, between the prosaic and the magical. When Kwan as Nunumu first hears Miss Banner's life story told in fractured stumbling Chinese, she forms the impression that Miss Banner has come from a peculiarly skewed and topsy-turvy universe. Miss Banner's little brothers chase a chicken into a deep hole and fall all the way to the other side of the world; her father picks scented money that grows like flowers and makes people happy; her mother puffs out her neck like a rooster, calls for her sons, and climbs down the hole that has swallowed them. After her mother's disappearance, Miss Banner's father takes her first to a palace governed by little Jesuses, and later to an island ruled by mad dogs. At length, the father vanishes and Miss Banner lives with a succession of uncles including one who cuts off pieces of China and sails off on a floating island. The reality—which Kwan learns after Miss Banner becomes more fluent in Chinese—is that Miss Banner's brothers died of chicken pox and her mother of a goiter disease; her father was an opium trader who put her in a school for Jesus-worshipping children in India; father and daughter left India for Malacca; and the uncles were actually a series of lovers. Tan's clever juxtaposition of fact and whimsy complements the surrealism that pervades the entire novel and validates for the reader the simultaneous existence of twentieth century and nineteenth century, Chinese and American, Kwan and Nunumu, and the *yin* people in Tan's fictional universe.

Tan also employs multiple versions of a story to create uncertainty and to describe a world in which no definite answers are possible. Jack Yee, the shadowy father that Kwan and Olivia barely remember, is an enigma to both daughters, but for different reasons. In Olivia's version of Jack's story—passed on to her by the American-born adults in the family—Jack was a good-looking university student in Guilin who was forced to marry a young market vendor when she became pregnant with his child. Five years later, when his wife died of a lung disease, the griefstricken Jack left his young daughter with an aunt and went to Hong Kong to begin a new life.

Before he could send for his beloved daughter, the Communist takeover in China destroyed all hope for a reunion between father and child, and the despondent Jack emigrated to America. Kwan's arrival replaces the sad story with an even more disturbing one. According to Kwan, her mother did not die of a lung disease; she died of "heartsickness" when her husband abandoned her with a four-year-old daughter and another child on the way. Kwan tells Olivia that all the water in her mother's belly "poured out as tears from her eyes. . . . That poor starving baby in her belly ate a hole in my mother's heart, and they both died." In this way, years later, Olivia learns what Kwan has always known. Their father had no legal or hereditary claim to the name Jack Yee. The name belonged to the owner of a stolen overcoat that the young university student who became their father purloined from a drunken man who had been trying to sell it for whatever cash he could get. In the coat's pockets were immigration permits, academic records, notification of admission to an American university, a ticket for passage on a ship, and cash—documents that would facilitate a new life in a wealthy country full of opportunity, far away from poverty, factory work, a pregnant wife, and a child. Donning the coat and the spectacles he found in one pocket, and appropriating the documents, the student became Jack Yee. But Amy Tan does not privilege Kwan's version. Kwan, in fact, prefaces her tale by saying that she heard it from Li Bin-bin, her mother's sister who raised her—and who, under the circumstances, would be unlikely to feel kindly toward the bogus Jack Yee. Thus the question remains: Who is the man behind the identity of Jack Yee? Kwan says that she has never known his true name, and she clearly knows almost nothing of his origins. And by extension, then, who are Olivia and Kwan? Who are their true ancestors? And who are Miss Banner and Nunumu? And, ultimately, how are all of these individuals connected?

Finally, Tan employs the many-layered triple narrative to interrogate the accounts of actual historical events, perhaps even to suggest that such accounts are unstable because they are the productions of gendered, class-defined, or racially constructed language. The Taiping Rebellion of the mid-nineteenth century is well known to Sinologists as well as to historians and geographers, but the standard texts tend toward factual Westernized accounts of military battles, descriptions of territory gained or lost, and tallies of victories and defeats. Kwan's version of the Rebellion privileges the perspective of a half-blind orphan who notices far more than battles between Manchu and Hakka. For one-eyed Nunumu, the Rebellion means the loss of her entire family, and life in a deserted village populated only by the elderly and the very young, the physically and mentally disabled, and the cowardly; the Heavenly King and his armies succeed only in bringing her hunger and cold, and a life of servitude in a house full of missionaries. Nunumu's experiences factor the personal element into a historical equation, revealing the frequently overlooked truth that military and political battles are always won or lost at the expense of thousands of individuals whose lives are forever disrupted by the ambitions of a powerful minority and their followers.

NARRATIVE POINT OF VIEW

The Hundred Secret Senses has two narrators: Olivia and Kwan. Olivia, from whose point of view the novel is structured, provides the frame story—an autobiographical narrative about her California childhood, her marriage, and her relationship with her older half-sister who emigrated to the United States when Olivia was a small child. Within the context of Olivia's story, Kwan speaks about her own life, telling stories about her colorful past, giving shape to her personal histories, giving voice to events that connect people and relationships between centuries and continents.

As Olivia narrates her own story, she reveals that at the core of her identity lie angst and unhappiness, doubts and skepticism. In Olivia's version of events, life has been one long series of rejections—first by her father who "abandons" her by dying when she is only four years old, then by her mother whose energy is consumed by a succession of boyfriends, and finally by Simon who appears never to have come to terms with the loss of his first love. Having decided that she needs her mother's complete attention as well as Simon's undiluted love, and having finally, grudgingly, decided that she will probably receive neither, Olivia is blind to Kwan's genuine affection, failing to appreciate the gift of love that her half-sister wants to bestow on her. As an adult, Olivia is constantly plagued by guilt whenever she is irritated by Kwan's ebullient attentions, and she worries because she feels incapable of reciprocating Kwan's unflagging loyalty.

Olivia's tendency to assume that she has been rejected influences not only her interpretation of the events of her life but also her assessment of Kwan's and Simon's places in her world. She is unable to accept Kwan's unconditional love or to believe that Simon genuinely loves her and not the ghost of the dead Elza. Olivia brushes off affectionate gestures from Kwan and Simon, or misreads their words and actions, wondering suspiciously why they refuse to leave her life, armoring herself in a casual attitude that she believes makes her impervious to further rejection. Her stories are well-chosen and cleverly constructed, her remarks intelligent, glib, witty, flip, but her insecurity colors her voice, making her sound occasionally petulant, frequently self-pitying, even maudlin.

The other major voice in the novel is Kwan's—a strong, memorable voice that is notable for its pragmatism as well as for its imagery. Although the novel is Olivia's story, Kwan gradually takes over with her distinctive talk story blend of travel narrative, legend, folktale, wry observation, and misremembered or reconstructed history as she attempts to make Olivia understand and finally acknowledge that they have a history together that goes back over a century.

If Olivia is skeptical and full of self-doubt, Kwan has a voice that embodies faith and total confidence in the universe and in herself. She believes in the World of *Yin*, she believes in second chances, she believes television commercials, and she certainly believes in her own abilities. Kwan cheerfully takes people to task for risking their health, dispenses her own versions of herbal lore and remedies, and offers unsolicited advice on sundry aspects of life from mending shattered crockery to patching up broken relationships. In fact, Kwan is so perfectly sure of her fluency in English that she corrects her husband: "Not *stealed*. . . . *Stolened*." She is equally certain about the soundness of the advice offered by her *yin* friends, and at one point she announces to the disbelieving Olivia that Lao Lu, a friend from the Taiping days and now a *yin* person, has decreed that Olivia and Simon must remain married because their fates are forever intertwined.

Kwan has two separate and distinctive voices. The voice in which she carries on her everyday conversations is an immigrant's, characterized by her use of the Chinese American patois to negotiate with verve and surety the daily transactions of her life. Her other voice, which has the cadences and rhythms of myth, legend, and folktale, transports Olivia—and the reader—into another world and another time. Through this fluent voice with its haunting images and sensory details, Kwan brings to life the story of the friendship between Nunumu and Miss Banner. Although Kwan's immigrant voice irritates Olivia, the poetic voice soothes, cajoles, resonates, and influences, leading Olivia to wonder, "So which part was her dream, which part was mine? Where did they intersect?"

CHARACTER DEVELOPMENT

The Hundred Secret Senses is about the lives of two distinct groups of major characters from different centuries and different cultures. Dominating the novel through their position in the framing twentieth-century American narrative are Olivia, her half-sister Kwan, and her husband Simon, while in the nineteenth-century Chinese stories told by Kwan are Nunumu, Miss Banner, and Yiban. Scores of other characters populate the world of the novel, adding color, action, and variety.

In her late thirties, Olivia is a thoroughly contemporary Californian—Berkeley graduate, professional photographer, more yuppie than Chinese. With a Chinese father and a mother who describes herself as "American mixed grill, a bit of everything white, fatty, and fried," Olivia seems overly conscious of her appearance, especially because she is sure that her name—Olivia Laguni—is completely at odds with her Asian features. Within her family, Olivia has always been compared with her Chinese father whose appearance and personality she is said to have inherited; an aunt frequently points out the fact that Olivia does not gain weight as her father did not, and her mother points out her tendency to be analytical, supposedly because she has her father's "accountant mentality."

As a child, Olivia was embarrassed by Kwan, who on arrival in the United States was too different from anyone Olivia had ever encountered. Kwan was too Chinese, too alien, too un-American in her behavior. Now an adult, Olivia is still embarrassed by Kwan, but with the wisdom of maturity, she also feels guilty about her attitude. Uncomfortably, Olivia admits that over the years she has not been kind or accepting to Kwan, refusing as a little girl to play with her odd sister, yelling derisively at her, and telling lies to avoid spending much time with her. "I've done nothing to endear myself to her," says Olivia, baffled by Kwan's insistent loyalty.

After years of listening to Kwan's stories and trying not to credit them, Olivia publicly projects a skeptical persona although inwardly she continues to worry about whether Kwan might be right about the existence of *yin* people. Olivia still is uncomfortable when she recalls that as a child she was able to see Kwan's invisible friends, and she constantly searches for ways to prove that her early experiences were the result of a child's imagination run riot. "I was pretending," she wails when Kwan reminds her that she has not always been an unbeliever. "Ghosts come from the imagination, not the World of Yin." Olivia's skepticism also is a function of her deeply felt conviction that she is unworthy of love. She believes that her mother and Simon have never loved her sufficiently. As a consequence, she finds it difficult to acknowledge Kwan's unconditional love or to accept Simon's genuine passion for her—and she conceals her doubts behind a bright skepticism tinged with suspicion.

Readers and critics have noted that Kwan is one of Amy Tan's most delightful and memorable character creations. On first meeting her new half-sister at the San Francisco Airport, Olivia gets the impression of a loud, extroverted, odd little person, short and chubby and badly dressed. That first image proves indelibly accurate; on further acquaintance, Kwan proves to be "a tiny dynamo . . . a miniature bull in a china shop." Moreover, Kwan never quite understands the principles that supposedly govern Western fashion, and she embarrasses Olivia by appearing in public in an outfit of turquoise trousers paired with a purple checked jacket.

Completely enamored of the United States and her new family, Kwan sets out to experience her new life with huge enthusiasm. So indiscriminately does she embrace all things American that Olivia's brother Tommy remarks that Kwan "believes in free speech, free association, free car wash with fill-'er'-up." Kwan's delight in her new siblings turns her into the family babysitter and surrogate mother, and Louise Laguni cheerfully relinquishes all responsibility to Kwan. Olivia's childhood memories all feature Kwan in the maternal roles that should have been played by Louise: when Olivia is taken ill at school, Kwan picks her up and brings her home; when Olivia weeps over some childhood disappointment, Kwan comforts her.

Kwan is a bit out of the ordinary in many ways, some of which defy explanation. She cannot come within three feet of a television without its hissing, and she has refused to wear a watch since the day she strapped on a digital watch and the numbers commenced to change rapidly like slot machine icons. After two hours, the watch stopped running permanently. Clearly, watches do not function properly on Kwan's wrist. Another peculiarity is the fact that without any electrical training, Kwan is able to pinpoint the source of a problem in an electrical circuit. In addition, she can reactivate a nonfunctioning cordless phone temporarily by pressing on the recharger nodes. Kwan clearly—and mysteriously—has a profound effect on things electrical and electronic, although she does nothing to precipitate appliances' strange reactions to her proximity.

Kwan's most distinctive characteristic is her regular conversations with people who are already dead. "I have yin eyes," she tells Olivia one night. "I can see yin people." When Olivia sleepily demands an explanation, Kwan informs her that *yin* people are those who have already died. Although Kwan appears to have visitors from all sectors of the World of *Yin* and speaks with a multitude of *yin* people, her most talkative and opinionated contact from that invisible world is Lao Lu, who, like Kwan, lived with and worked for the missionaries who inhabited the Ghost Merchant's house in nineteenth-century Changmian. Kwan claims that her ability to converse with the *yin* people is the result of her highly developed "hundred secret senses," which she describes as similar to "ant feet, elephant trunk, dog nose, cat whisker, whale ear, bat wing, clam shell, snake tongue, little hair on flower." She tells Olivia that the hundred secret senses resemble the other senses, other modes of knowing, other avenues from the outside world into the soul. These secret senses are the keys to Kwan's certitude about life; they are her connections to other lives.

Another of Kwan's unique traits is her determined persistence.

Although the young Olivia has assiduously avoided learning to speak Chinese, Kwan insinuates language lessons into her nightly conversations with the child, telling fascinating stories in Chinese, with the result that Olivia learns the language unconsciously and with little effort. "She pushed her Chinese secrets into my brain," Olivia recalls, adding that her worldview has been immeasurably altered by her association with Kwan. Years later, when Olivia and Simon initiate divorce proceedings, Kwan determinedly maneuvers them into traveling to China with her because she is convinced that their true destiny awaits them in that country. Olivia finds Kwan's persistence particularly trying, especially Kwan's dogged determination to be loyal to her no matter how she behaves toward Kwan; despite countless rebuffs, Kwan cheerily persists in remaining an important component of Olivia's life.

Olivia's husband, Simon Bishop, is a more sympathetic—and somewhat more fully developed—character than most of the male characters in Tan's other novels. Differing from the cardboard figures or nearly invisible men of *The Joy Luck Club*, men who tend to be patriarchal authority figures or male nonentities, or the brutal Wen Fu in *The Kitchen God's Wife*, Simon is more multifaceted, very much a product of the late twentieth century. He is a man who mourns the death of his first love, who argues with Olivia over custody of a Yorkshire terrier–Chihuahua mixed breed dog, and who is not too proud to accept a dinner invitation from Kwan if it is the only strategy that will allow him to remain connected with Olivia. Although he helped to write the proposal for the travel article about Chinese cuisine, he offers to give up the China trip if Olivia thinks that she might be more comfortable traveling with another writer. Unlike the men in other Tan novels, Simon is neither monster nor detached observer; he is, instead, a vulnerable man who seems puzzled and even hurt by Olivia's request for a divorce.

Like Olivia, Simon has a multiethnic background, which includes a Chinese ancestor; unlike Olivia, he is far less Chinese and more definitively Western. While Olivia grew up in and around Chinese communities, Simon spent his childhood in Utah. He, in fact, identifies himself as Hawaiian, although Kwan claims to see a resemblance between him and her sister, saying at one point that Olivia and Simon look like twins. Nevertheless, as attractive as he is, Simon remains far less interesting than the women characters, and, in fact, lacks even the vignette brilliance of minor characters like Zeng, the one-eared peddler; Rocky, the ambitious taxi driver in Guilin; or Du Lili, Kwan's elderly friend in Changmian.

Kwan's dream-like stories about her previous existence are focused on the linked lives of two women: Nunumu, the Hakka girl that Kwan claims is herself in a previous life, and Nelly Banner, the American woman to whom Nunumu gives her complete loyalty and, finally, her life. So vivid are Kwan's narratives, so compelling are the episodes that she recounts, that the novel becomes as much the story of Nunumu and Miss Banner as it is the story of Kwan and Olivia.

Nunumu occupies the center of Kwan's stories about life with the Jesus Worshippers. Orphaned in the mass enthusiasm for the Taiping cause, Nunumu is one-eyed, the result of a childhood injury from a falling rock, but she is courageous and resourceful. She eventually makes her way from her devastated home village to Jintian and then into the household of the missionaries where she works as a servant and as Miss Banner's companion. Nunumu teaches Miss Banner to speak Chinese and becomes her confidante, and after six years during which their friendship grows and strengthens, they flee together into the mountains in a vain attempt to escape the marauding Manchu soldiers.

Nelly Banner is a drifter. American by birth, she spent part of her childhood in India and Malacca, and after her father died, she lived with a succession of lovers before she found herself abandoned by the latest lover in Canton where she met the English missionaries and began traveling with them. When Nunumu saves Miss Banner from drowning, the two women's lives become entwined, and with her heroic act, Nunumu takes on the responsibility for Miss Banner's life and well-being. Kwan tells Olivia that because of the rescue, Nunumu's and Miss Banner's lives had "flowed together in that river, and became as tangled and twisted as a drowned woman's hair."

Through the novel parades an astonishingly vivid collection of minor characters, none of them completely developed, but all of them distinctively rendered and memorable. The best of these fantastic figures inhabit Kwan's stories about Nunumu's life in the Ghost Merchant's house: pompous and deceitful General Cape with his military costumes; half-Chinese and half-American Yiban, driven by his devotion to Miss Banner; nervous Miss Mouse; fervent Pastor Amen; opium-eating Dr. Too Late. But no less attention-getting are some of the dramatis personae from Kwan's twentieth-century childhood: Buncake who never speaks but only waves her hands and carols "Lili lili" in a high voice; Du Yun who is so overcome with grief that she imagines she has become her dead adopted daughter; Third Auntie, the clairvoyant who explains to Li Bin-bin and Du Lili why Kwan and Buncake appear to have become one and the same little girl; and finally, the nameless young girls who struggle up a steep mountain to set birds free in return for wishes come true.

SETTING

Setting in *The Hundred Secret Senses* serves to highlight the geographical backgrounds and cultural realities of Kwan's life, as well as the rich dual heritage that Olivia and Simon share as American-born Chinese. Like Tan's two earlier books, the novel is set in America and China—two locations that are separated temporally and spatially, culturally and historically—but unlike those two novels, *Secret Senses* also attempts to identify connections and draw parallels between two centuries.

Olivia's San Francisco is a thoroughly American metropolis, a late-twentieth-century urban environment that embraces equally a motley assortment of inhabitants: free-lance artists and writers; the Market Street eccentric who loudly prophesies to passers-by that California will one day slide into the ocean "like a plate of clams"; people walking dogs on the trails of the Presidio; AIDS patients; women who regularly spend their time at spas; Chinese immigrants caught between the Old World and the New. Geographically, the novel's San Francisco encompasses Golden Gate Park (where Olivia and Simon are married in an outdoor ceremony), Chinatown and Balboa Street, the Sunset district, and Pacific Heights, on the fringes of which Olivia and Simon have purchased a co-op apartment in a renovated Victorian house. Although Kwan has been a San Francisco resident for over thirty years, the city has never become her natural landscape. She moves through the city and its neighborhoods with the ease of a long-time resident, sniffing out sales at "Emporium Capwell," chatting with long-time customers at the drugstore where she works, arguing with a veterinarian over a bill; but China remains her constant point of reference, and Olivia notices that Kwan has recently begun to mention China in nearly every conversation.

Half a world away from San Francisco, twentieth-century Changmian seems to be almost a Chinese Brigadoon, unchanged and picturesque despite the major political and ideological upheavals. Olivia's first glimpse of Changmian reveals to her a landscape straight out of a glossy travel poster, a scene that in reality has been photographed and displayed in glossy magazines countless times. She sees a rural community nestled at the base of two jagged karst peaks with vivid green forested flanks. The village itself consists of rows of whitewashed houses with tile roofs, and surrounding the houses are carefully tended fields and ponds bisected and intersected with stone walls and irrigation canals. Olivia immediately falls under the seductive spell of the village, feeling that she has discovered "a fabled misty land, half memory, half illusion," and she realizes with surprise that Changmian is a familiar landscape, the setting for the stories that Kwan insinuated into her dreams time and again years before. Changmian is Kwan's emotional and psychological homeland, the native landscape of her lives, and the place to which she must finally return to fulfill her dreams. And despite her thirty-year absence and a full life in a completely different culture and landscape, Kwan slips unobtrusively, seamlessly back into the domestic routine at Big Ma's and Du Lili's house in the village.

Kwan's narratives also reveal another Changmian, a village that during the Taiping years is an impoverished enclave in a valley below rugged limestone mountains tunneled with hundreds of caves through which the wind blows incessantly. From the garden of the Ghost Merchant's house, Nunumu can see the village houses below as well as the stone archway that leads into the next valley, and further away, the mountains where she once roamed as a child; but her daily existence is now defined by the walls that enclose the house, its overgrown garden, and the pavilion where the previous owner is said to have died. For six years, Nunumu's circumscribed life within those walls reflects her position as a servant to the missionaries who inhabit the house and grounds. For five days each week, she washes and irons the missionaries' clothing, mends torn garments, cooks, and cleans. On Sundays, like all of the other servants and many of the village people, she is required to attend long worship services conducted by Pastor Amen. Only on Saturdays does Nunumu venture beyond the garden walls, and then only in the company of Miss Banner to distribute religious tracts to the inhabitants of Changmian.

Throughout the novel, Changmian displays two faces: one face presents the magical timeless village of Kwan's edited memories and Olivia's first impressions; the other face belongs to the poor but vibrant community that proudly—and joyously—sends its best and strongest citizens to fight for the cause of the Heavenly King in the Taiping wars, and a century later participates with equal enthusiasm in the frenzied rush to cash in on a significant archaeological discovery—the luminous underground lake and prehistoric village that come to light during the search for Kwan in the mountain caves. In all of its incarnations, Changmian is the setting for Kwan's epic narrative of love and loss and rebirth—and both Changmians become the sites of Olivia's journey toward self. The mythic, timeless village calls Olivia back from twentieth-century California to the ancient landscape that witnessed the flowering of love between Yiban and Miss Banner; but it is in the primitive village with mud streets and lively chattering people that Olivia begins the process of reconnection with her psyche and then with Simon.

LITERARY DEVICES

So adept is Amy Tan's handling of figurative language, so precise is her choice of words and her crafting of verbal pictures, that memorable characters and thematically significant settings come to life in the novel. Through her use of symbol clusters and images, Tan creates fictional stages on which her characters play their roles, enacting the conflicts through which Tan explores the power of memory and the nature of relationships.

Sometimes whimsical, other times evocative, occasionally surreal, chapter titles reiterate the novel's themes, foreshadowing and calling attention to the images and symbols that ornament the text. Images summoned by the titles serve to reinforce the sense of otherworldliness, the mystery of Kwan's stories: "The Girl with the Yin Eyes," "The Ghost Merchant's House," "The Catcher of Ghosts," even "When Light Balances with Dark." Other titles suggest temporality, important events and everyday occurrences, the passage of time: "The Funeral," "Hello Goodbye," "Kwan's Fiftieth," "The Year of No Flood"; still others prefigure the novel's food imagery: "Kwan's Kitchen," "The Best Time to Eat Duck Eggs," or "Six-Roll Spring Chicken."

Miss Banner's music box plays a significant role in the Changmian years and thus in Kwan's stories, as well as later, in Olivia's experiences. The box, a gift to Miss Banner from her father, is a safe hiding place for her diary and assorted keepsakes. During worship services, the missionaries use the box to accompany their singing although they have had to write new words to accompany the tune, which is inappropriate because it is a German drinking song. When Miss Banner attempts to elope with General Cape, Nunumu buries the box, symbolically obliterating all memories of her friend who has—Nunumu feels—betrayed their friendship. After Miss Banner returns and falls in love with Yiban, Nunumu unearths the box and restores it to its owner. Months later, with the missionaries dead and the clear threat of danger surrounding the Ghost Merchant's house, Miss Banner and Nunumu carefully pack the music box with mementos and reminders of their dead companions—a pill bottle, a glove, a button, a travel book, a tin of special tea. They light candles, turn the key to play the music box, and listen to the tinkling notes of the familiar melody—and in that way, they perform a homely funeral service for their dead friends. When the comforting ritual is over, they flee, carrying the box, to the cave in the mountains where Nunumu has left Yiban waiting for Miss Banner.

In those very mountains a century later, Olivia watches as Kwan pries open a reddish wooden box trimmed in brass. When she lifts the lid, the lilting high-pitched sounds of a martial melody emanate from the box, and

Kwan removes from the box a kidskin glove, a small book—*A Visit to India, China, and Japan*—with deckled edges, a small tin, a journal with notes about unfamiliar food and snippets of information about the Taiping followers. The journal is dated 1859, and Olivia remembers Kwan's bedtime stories about a year identified as *Yi ba liu si*, the Chinese words for 1864. Kwan's Nunumu stories are set in 1864, just five years after the journal's date, and Olivia realizes that it is just possible for Miss Banner to have owned the volume. Struggling with her need for logical explanations, Olivia is forced to ask herself some crucial questions about Kwan's stories, especially about the reasons why Kwan has been so insistent that Olivia listen attentively to those stories—and at that moment, on that mountain, Olivia experiences an epiphany. She realizes that she has always known somehow, instinctively, why Kwan persists in telling story after story about Nunumu and Miss Banner; however, Olivia has resisted acknowledging her awareness of Kwan's reasons. Over the years, Kwan has asked, "Libby-ah, you remember?" And Olivia has denied, both to herself and to Kwan, any memory, knowing as she disclaims all knowledge of the past, that Kwan is hoping to hear her say "of course I remember. I was Miss Banner." As Olivia and Kwan turn over the tangible evidence of the truth of Kwan's stories about the Ghost Merchant's house, Olivia realizes that she can no longer deny that she and Kwan might indeed have had a shared history that began a century before Kwan's arrival at the San Francisco airport.

The major symbol group in the novel involves food in all its guises, its preparation, its consumption, its significance. Food becomes a literary language; gastronomic images and motifs provide Kwan with the means of re-creating her life as Nunumu in the last days of the Taiping regime, as well as with the words to re-create the story of Buncake, the little girl whose body Kwan appropriated long ago after the floods. Food also functions as a symbol for the intensity of the culture shock that Olivia and Simon experience when they travel to China with Kwan. And in the end, food for Olivia comes to represent Kwan's nurturing presence—and Olivia's own salvation.

Attempting to nudge Olivia into overcoming her skepticism and traveling with her into the memory of their life together in the Ghost Merchant's house, Kwan conjures up vivid recollections of the food and meals that she remembers from that existence. She contrasts the lavish Western breakfasts consumed by the missionaries during the peaceful years of plenty, with the sparse scavenged dinners that mark the years of starvation during the conflict between Manchu and Taiping. Bacon and eggs, corn cakes and fruit give way to fried locusts and grasshoppers, frogs and bats, that Nunumu and Lao Lu identify for the missionaries as "rabbit" so as not to disgust the squeamish Western palates. But although food imagery can be a powerful aid to the recovery of buried memories, Kwan's recollections of these distinctive meals do not evoke any answering reminiscences from Olivia, who listens politely and even interestedly, but disclaims any memory of the meals that Kwan is describing in such detail.

One especially notable food motif is preserved duck eggs, which for Kwan symbolize Nunumu's subversive resourcefulness. Because she loves duck eggs so much, Nunumu steals eggs—one or two at a time—from the missionaries, although she is careful to point out that they prefer chicken eggs to duck eggs. Nunumu preserves the eggs in quantities of precious salt to which she has free access because she supposedly needs the salt for removing stains from the weekly laundry. She coats the salted eggs in mud, and stores them in cracked pottery jars for which she barters some of her precious eggs. The preserved duck eggs represent security for Nunumu, who eventually squirrels away ten rows of jars full of eggs, and the eggs become the missionaries' sustenance when food supplies run short during the Manchu wars with the Taiping kingdom. The eggs also create the opportunity for Nunumu to experience her own romance when Zeng, the peddler who supplies her with jars in exchange for eggs, decides that he wants her to become his wife. For Nunumu, the first hint of Zeng's courtship surfaces when he offers to give her an unblemished jar even when she has no eggs to trade because the missionaries have eaten most of them.

Amy Tan also uses food imagery as a characterization device. When Kwan recounts the story of Buncake, Kwan's description of Du Yun's skillful preparation of fried frogs provides a painful parallel to Buncake's recollections of how her mother and father died. Buncake, who has been orphaned by the early "re-education" efforts that swept China just before the total communist take-over, is taken in by Kwan's aunt, Du Yun, a woman who prides herself on one special culinary creation—freshly killed frogs, quickly sauteed in hot oil until they are crisp. As Du Yun deftly skins and dismembers the frogs, she fails to notice that Buncake is cowering silently behind Kwan with her fist jammed into her mouth "like a sandbag stopping a leak in a riverbank." Speechless, Buncake is unable to explain to Du Yun that the scene is horrifically distressing, that "this tearing of skin from flesh" reminds her of how her mother and father had died while she watched from the tree in which her father had hidden her. Buncake has not spoken since then because her last promise to her mother had been that she would be quiet and not say a word or make a sound.

For Olivia and Simon, food symbolizes the profound dislocation that they experience in China. The trip is originally conceived as a journalistic odyssey during which they would work on a free-lance project for a travel and food magazine. "We would offer to write and photograph a story on village cuisine of China," recalls Olivia, adding that their grand dreams included other similar articles, a book and lecture tour, even a TV series. When they finally are persuaded to accompany Kwan to China, Olivia and Simon envision taking exotic photographs and writing evocative text, and they arrive in Guilin ready to avail themselves of every possible photo opportunity. At first, they are not disappointed, for they breakfast on freshly cooked pancakes from a street vendor as they stroll past colorful displays of fruit and other produce, as well as a variety of other wares for sale. As Olivia focuses a photograph of a bustling street market, Simon makes notes for the accompanying text and scouts around the stalls for other photographic possibilities. At the bird market, Olivia is fascinated by a beautiful white owl with eyes that remind her of chocolate. Sensing her interest, the seller offers Olivia and Simon the owl with the suggestion that they take it to a nearby restaurant to be butchered and cooked for their evening meal. The two are, predictably disturbed. Protesting when Kwan begins a spirited round of haggling with the bird seller, and visibly upset when Kwan purchases the owl, Olivia is not appeased until she discovers that Kwan's intent is to climb a mountain and release the owl so that it can fly from a mountaintop carrying Kwan's wishes. What Olivia does not yet know is that the true test of their capacity to stomach the strange and the unfamiliar awaits them in Changmian at the home where Kwan grew up.

Fascinated by Olivia's camera, Kwan's family friend, Du Lili, goes out of her way to stage interesting photographic subjects, at one point slashing a chicken's neck and then letting the bird stumble around on the ground until it falls dead. As she dismembers the chicken and then cooks it in its own blood, she chatters about how she has intentionally prolonged the butchering to give Olivia a more interesting subject to photograph. Appalled, Olivia worries about dinner, having finally confronted the tremendous difference between her expectations about China and the realities with which she is confronted. After watching Du Lili, Olivia finds the chicken stew unappetizing at best, but she also knows that there is nothing else that she can eat, "no ham and cheese in the fridge—there's no fridge!" Because they are hungry, she and Simon tentatively try the chicken, and to their surprise, they find the stew flavorful. Before the evening is over, they also have imbibed "pickle-mouse wine," which displays at the bottom of the wine bottle a grayish object with a tail. The old Olivia of just a week earlier would have been sickened at the idea of drinking any liquid in which a mouse has been preserved—in fact, she is silently wondering why she does not feel the need to vomit. Instead, she and Simon burst out in uncontrollable laughter, apprehension giving way to catharsis, possibly because at that point they understand that this meal has been their gastronomic initiation—and they have not only survived but triumphed over their inhibitions and preconceptions. They have progressed far beyond their initial idea of superficial travelogue articles with glossy photographs to an authentic home-cooked Chinese meal in a genuine Chinese village. Moreover, they have thoroughly enjoyed the experience and are suffused with feelings of well-being.

Food for Kwan is a form of nurturing communication, the language of love and acceptance through which she continues her efforts to bond with Olivia. When she finds twelve-year-old Olivia weeping, Kwan immediately assumes that little Olivia has consumed more than her share of the Christmas cookies that Kwan has baked and is suffering from a stomachache. To Kwan, the solution is simple—she will decrease the sugar in the next batch of cookies so that Olivia can eat as many as she wants. Worrying years later about Olivia who looks unhappy and exhausted in the weeks following her separation from Simon, Kwan invites her to dinner, promising that the menu will include Olivia's favorite dish, potstickers, and indicating that a supply of wontons will be available for Olivia's freezer. For another dinner, Kwan offers Olivia dried scallops, a rare and precious delicacy that costs an astonishing sixty dollars per pound. Unfortunately, despite her enjoyment of Kwan's excellent cooking, Olivia repeatedly fails to decode the messages of love and sisterly concern that Kwan conveys through her offerings of food.

At the end of the novel, food becomes Olivia's salvation, revealing to her in rather dramatic fashion the unbreakable connections between the past and the present. Standing in a drizzle with the small group of mourners at Big Ma's grave, Olivia watches as Du Lili places a preserved duck egg into Big Ma's hand before the coffin is lowered into the ground. The sight of the egg awakens in Olivia the memory of Nunumu's cache of preserved duck eggs, and before she is completely aware of what she is doing, she races to the ruins of the Ghost Merchant's house and begins to dig frantically near where she thinks the old garden wall might once have stood. Her efforts soon reveal a pottery jar that she immediately breaks open with the handle of her hoe. From that jar, she extracts one age-darkened egg after another, cradling the fragile muddy eggs to her chest against which they crumble and disintegrate. For Olivia, the eggs are "relics of [her] past disintegrating into gray chalk," but she is unperturbed at the loss of the eggs: "I knew I had already tasted what was left." If Olivia has needed any further evidence to support Kwan's reminiscences, she has that evidence lying before her in the muddy trench that she has dug in the Ghost Merchant's garden: the eggs are the final corroboration that Kwan's stories are records of real events and real individuals; each crumbling egg is the ultimate proof of connections and resonances between one life and the next, between one continent and another one on the other side of the globe.

CULTURAL AND HISTORICAL CONTEXTS

A fairly substantial portion of *The Hundred Secret Senses* is set in nineteenth-century China—more specifically in the 1850s and 1860s during the Taiping Rebellion, the most important peasant-led revolt in Chinese history. The Taiping regime, led by the charismatic Hong Xiuquan, gained strength during the Qing Dynasty in the wake of the opium wars, the opening of China's borders to foreign trade, and the loss of Hong Kong to the British crown. At its height, the rebellion involved over 600,000 men and 500,000 women. Borrowing their ideology and teachings from Christianity, the Taiping followers rebelled against what they considered to be corruption and obsolescence in the imperial court, demanding widespread changes that included equality for women, agricultural reform, and the abolition of private property.

Educated in part by Western missionaries whose teachings apparently resonated with his own naturally mystical leanings, Hong Xiuquan converted to Christianity, and thereafter claimed not only that he was Jesus Christ's younger brother, but also that his relationship to Jesus made him the Heavenly King on earth. He recruited thousands of followers from the peasant classes by announcing his intention to create *Taiping tianguo*, or "a Heavenly Kingdom of Great Peace" in which the faithful would labor together for the good of the community. In this kingdom, everyone would have equal access to education, and footbinding and slavery would be outlawed. In addition, undesirable habits such as gambling, drinking alcohol, and smoking tobacco would be forbidden.

The Heavenly Kingdom flourished until 1864 in Nanjing, which had become its capital. During that summer, two provincial armies, financed by a coalition of the French, the British, and the Qing government, marched into Nanjing. When he realized that he could not defend his "kingdom" against the superior might of the massed European and Chinese forces, Hong Xiuquan committed suicide. Rather than surrendering, his men followed suit. A few weeks later, Nanjing fell to the invading armies, and the Heavenly Kingdom ceased to exist.

Amy Tan has chosen to identify Nunumu/Kwan with a distinctive minority ethnic Chinese group whose name, Hakka, which means "foreigner," was originally a pejorative label for the ethnic peoples who migrated from northern China to settle in the southern provinces. Because Hong Xiuquan was of Hakka origin, and also because the Taiping regime advocated equality for women and banned foot-binding and prostitution, Nunumu and her people—the Hakka—are attracted to the teachings of the Heavenly King and are eager to join the rebellion. Like the Taiping rebels, the Hakka were known for their egalitarian leanings, and Hakka women—famed for their industry, cleverness, and physical strength—never bound their feet, even during the Qing period when that custom was followed most rigidly. The independent Hakka found it difficult to gain acceptance from the peoples through whose lands they traveled. Speaking of her past life as Nunumu, Kwan says, "We were . . . Guest People—hnh!—meaning guests not invited to stay in any good place too long." Because Nunumu is a one-eyed Hakka girl, she is an outsider. She has marginal status in China because of her ethnic heritage, in the Ghost Merchant's house because she is a Chinese servant in a household of Westerners, in the population at large because she is physically deformed. In San Francisco, Kwan is likewise marginal. Bob Laguni does not adopt her as he does Louise's children; consequently, Kwan never legally becomes a part of the family. And finally, despite decades of life in California, Kwan still has not truly assimilated into middle American culture. She retains her Chinese-English speech, continues to live in a Chinatown neighborhood, persists in dressing like an immigrant, and still dreams of one day returning to China.

THEMES AND MAJOR ISSUES

Like Amy Tan's first two novels, *The Hundred Secret Senses* explores a number of issues that have become familiar to Tan's readers: family relationships—especially connections between generations, and the bonds between sisters; linguistic differences and miscommunication; identity; biculturalism, ethnicity, and the tensions of living between worlds; cultural dislocation; and women's roles. In this third novel, several new themes appear, among them love (in all its guises), loyalty, faith, and the unreliability of memory. Tan herself claims that the novel is about love, saying that *The Hundred Secret Senses* answers "a question about love, unconditional love." While authorial intent and reader reaction are not always congruent, it is abundantly clear that love is a dominant theme in the novel.

Several forms of love are enacted throughout the novel: Louise Laguni's numerous infatuations; General Cape's mercenary courtship of a Chinese banker's daughter as well as his lustful pursuit of Miss Banner; the steady affection between Kwan and George (and Nunumu and Zeng); Miss Mouse's unrequited adoration of Dr. Too Late. Meanwhile, at the center of the novel are Olivia and Simon, soulmates by Kwan's (and Lao Lu's) definition despite the couple's impending divorce. In Kwan's universe, Olivia and Simon are simply continuing a great romance that began in the waning months of the Taiping when they were Miss Banner and Yiban Johnson.

Complicating the central romance, however, is Olivia's belief that Simon still loves Elza who died before he met Olivia, and Simon's apparent inability to accept the finality of Elza's death suggests briefly the possibility of an obsessive love. Through the turmoil of the relationship between Olivia and Simon, Amy Tan examines love and its resilience, its capacity for enduring even beyond the ultimate separation, death; and she portrays the lengths to which human beings will go in search of love.

Tan also portrays another form of love that is as binding and enduring as romantic love—the love that forges unbreakable links between friends. This form of love, which is an intense combination of affection, respect, loyalty, and companionship, finds its clearest manifestation in the friendship between Nunumu and Miss Banner, and later in the unselfish sisterly love that Kwan offers to Olivia. During the trip to China, Kwan describes this kind of love as she remembers a fervent wish that she made before she left for America: "My first wish: to have a sister I could love with all my heart, only that, and I would ask for nothing more from her." When her wish for a sister is granted, Kwan enthusiastically keeps her promise; her affection for Olivia is boundless and requires no reciprocity.

Another theme that surfaces in *The Hundred Secret Senses* involves loyalty and its opposite, betrayal. Kwan embodies loyalty; in fact she uses the word "loyalty" frequently in her everyday conversation as well as in her stories. In Kwan's tales, the loyalty of Nunumu to Miss Banner is so intense that the former leaves the safety of her mountain hiding place to lead Miss Banner to safety, and when it becomes clear that the approaching soldiers will overtake them, Nunumu stays with Miss Banner and dies with her. Despite his betrayal of her, Nelly Banner remains loyal to General Cape until events force her to understand that he is using her to gain access to the missionaries' funds and food supplies. And Zeng, whose courtship of Nunumu is so prosaic as to seem offhanded, proves his loyalty to her by returning immediately after he is killed by the Manchu to lead Nunumu and Yiban to the safety of the mountain caves. Zeng then vanishes immediately after promising that he will wait for Nunumu forever. Kwan herself is so loyal to her sister that Olivia's mean jokes in childhood and snide remarks as an adult have not deflected Kwan's love. On the contrary, each time Olivia rebuffs her efforts, Kwan simply tries harder and more often to be of use, to be supportive, to be helpful, and above all, to love.

As a contrast to Kwan's (and Nunumu's) loyalty, Amy Tan has created the character of the villainous General Cape who personifies treachery and betrayal. Telling one of her stories, Kwan recalls, "General Cape, he was rotten too. He threw away other people." Cape abandons Miss Banner to marry the daughter of a wealthy banker, and when he is forced to flee after cuckolding the banker with the man's younger wives, Cape comes to Changmian to resume his affair with Miss Banner whose misplaced loyalty to him leads her to take him back. After staying with Miss Banner and the missionaries for two months, Cape disappears with the group's food supplies, pack animals, and mission money. When he reappears, he leads a gang of Manchu soldiers who lay waste to the countryside around Changmian. Cape and his men take over the Ghost Merchant's house, and when Lao Lu protests, they kill him.

The novel illustrates other and less dramatic forms of betrayal. At her husband's deathbed, Olivia's mother Louise vows never to remarry, and to spend the rest of her life honoring the name of Yee and the Chinese heritage that it represents. Yet within a short time, she has met and married Bob Laguni, and is raising completely assimilated American children who know next to nothing about Chinese culture. When she is a child, Olivia betrays Kwan by telling their parents that Kwan communicates with ghosts, and the alarmed parents promptly incarcerate Kwan in a mental hospital. As an adult, Olivia unthinkingly continues her betrayal of Kwan in small ways: pretending to be so busy that she cannot find the time to accept Kwan's invitations to dinner, giving Kwan only a token gift of an inexpensive faux tortoise-shell box at her big fiftieth-birthday celebration, never telephoning Kwan until the laundry basket is full and Olivia needs to use Kwan's washing machine. Despite these daily betrayals, Kwan loyally continues to refer to Olivia as her favorite sister, and Olivia continues to be overcome with guilt each time Kwan invites her to dinner, presents her with pre-cooked dinners for her freezer, or even telephones her.

In *The Hundred Secret Senses*, Amy Tan explores the theme of sisterhood—a departure from her earlier focus on mothers and daughters in her first two novels. Sisters are prominently featured in myth, folktale, and literature, frequently as rivals or antagonists, often as women estranged by birth order or parental favor. Cinderella and her ugly sisters, as well as King Lear's feuding daughters, are familiar examples of competition and conflict between sisters. Less generally familiar are Lizzie and Laura of Christina Rossetti's poem "Goblin Market"—sisters whose radically divergent attitudes toward life and experience separate them and threaten harm to Laura, until Lizzie's love for her sister leads her to risk death to save Laura. Unlike these traditional and literary treatments of sisterhood, Amy Tan chooses to focus on the ways in which sisters influence each other as they each work through the complicated process of defining a clear sense of self and a balanced identity.

In her study, *Psyche's Sisters: Re-Imagining the Meaning of Sisterhood*, Christine Downing points out that "the interactions among sisters . . .

instigate the heroine's journey toward self, toward psyche." She continues, "Our sisterly relationships challenge and nurture us, even as we sometimes disappoint and betray one another." *The Hundred Secret Senses* is primarily about Olivia's journey toward self and wholeness, and about the role that Kwan plays in Olivia's quest. From the time of her adored father's death when she was four years old, Olivia has felt unanchored, a feeling that has persisted into her adulthood, complicating every relationship she has had and rendering her incapable of freely accepting love. In the midst of Olivia's uncertainty, Kwan is the constant; Kwan, in fact, provides Olivia with a continuing long-lasting and stable human connection, although Olivia has never recognized the importance of Kwan's role in her life.

Before Kwan comes to San Francisco, Olivia at first mistakenly believes that she will be replaced when the new daughter arrives. Thus on hearing that Kwan will be an addition to the family rather than a replacement, Olivia is delighted, until she realizes that she will more than likely have to share her mother's limited time with the newcomer. Already feeling neglected by her mother, Olivia is in no mood to be forced into competition for attention. But not until Kwan is installed in the Laguni household does a worse possibility become obvious to Olivia: with Kwan in residence to look after the younger children, Louise Laguni has more time than ever to spend with her friends. As a consequence, Olivia has resented Kwan from the beginning for taking the place of the mother whose attention Olivia wanted desperately; and although Kwan capably performs the maternal role that Louise has abandoned, Olivia refuses to accept the substitution, rejecting Kwan's care and nurturance, and repudiating everything that Kwan represents.

The presence of Kwan in Olivia's life problematizes Olivia's relationship with and position in a cultural group to which she belongs by heritage—Asian Americans. For Olivia, Kwan represents ethnicity, a diaspora culture, and racial origins that comprise the visible half of Olivia's genetic inheritance and almost nothing of her cultural bias. Kwan is indelibly Other—she speaks with an accent and an incomplete command of English vocabulary, she wears odd clothes that mark her as an immigrant, and she claims regular communication with invisible correspondents from an insubstantial existence. By contrast, Olivia is all-American except for her Asian features; she dresses fashionably, and she is rational to a fault and skeptical as well. And yet, Kwan and Olivia are sisters; they share a father, and Kwan has been an important part of Olivia's life since the latter was a child.

Early in their relationship, young Olivia wants nothing to do with Chinese culture, which she equates with her strange new immigrant sister. She is embarrassed by her kinship with Kwan, playing cruel jokes on her that highlight their differences, and disclaiming any blood ties when neighborhood children taunt Kwan. As Olivia matures, her embarrassment gives way to guilt about her treatment of Kwan, and that guilt becomes a barrier to the development of any form of genuine companionship between the sisters. Yet despite Olivia's resistance and the unacknowledged gulf between them, Kwan has been responsible all along for anchoring Olivia in a community—although Olivia remains oblivious for years to the importance of the cultural context that she has acquired through her sister's insistent tutelage. Thanks to Kwan, Olivia speaks Chinese, knows late nineteenth-century Chinese history, and even identifies a Chinese dish as her favorite food. And when Olivia finally visits China and Kwan's native village for the first time, she is overwhelmed by the feeling that she has come home; and for the first time, she begins to feel her kinship with Kwan and to move toward integrating the elements of her heritage into a complete identity that includes the existence of a Chinese half-sister.

Like Olivia, Kwan needs sisterly help as she works to restore the harmony that has been absent from her life since she was Nunumu and told the lie that separated Yiban and Miss Banner. On one level, Kwan's stories about Nunumu and Miss Banner reflect her wistful hope that she and Olivia can forge strong ties of affection. The strength and persistence of her hopes become evident during the China journey when she remembers that as a young girl in Changmian, her greatest wish was to have a sister to love more than anyone else in the world. She admits having made a vow that if the wish were to come true, she would be perfectly content, never again wishing for anything else. On another level, Kwan's stories are prompts or hints that she hopes will remind Olivia of their common history; for only when Olivia is able to acknowledge their century-old connection will Kwan be able to absolve herself of her guilt.

In China, Olivia and Kwan are together again as they were when Olivia was a child, as they have not been in almost thirty years. In the geography that has shaped their lives, they re-establish their emotional connections with each other and they reaffirm a relationship that has endured through at least two lifetimes. More importantly, they are blessed with a rare opportunity: they are empowered to correct the mistakes of an earlier time, and as they rewrite their story, each one finds what she has been seeking—an integrated self for Olivia and peace for Kwan.

ALTERNATIVE READING: JUNGIAN ARCHETYPAL CRITICISM

Advocates of archetypal criticism, sometimes called myth criticism, theorize the existence of what Gilbert Murray has described as "the memory of the race, stamped, as it were, upon our physical organism."

This racial memory—the residue of some form of universal human experience—is manifested in and through archetypes, or narrative patterns, symbols, images, themes, and character types that recur in literature, art, religion, folklore, ritual, and particularly in myths and dreams. An archetypal critic examines the appearance of these universal patterns and symbols in a literary text, studying their contextual implications, and seeking to formulate conclusions about the functions of those archetypes in the work.

Archetypal criticism had its earliest beginnings in the results of fieldwork in primitive cultures done by British anthropologist Sir James George Frazer (1854–1941) whose research into ritual and magic among primitive peoples suggested to him the existence of recurrent narrative and ritual patterns common to widely dispersed cultures and societies. In his immense and influential comparison of mythologies, *The Golden Bough* (1890-1915), Frazer analyzes the parallels between the ritualistic patterns he had detected in primitive cultures and certain structural elements in myths, legends, and folktales. Although Frazer's work was eventually superseded— even disputed—by the work of later generations of anthropologists, his identification and documentation of seemingly universal patterns influenced some early twentieth-century literary critics, among them Gilbert Murray.

Even more important to the development of archetypal criticism is the work of Carl Gustav Jung, the Swiss psychiatrist and the founder of analytical psychology, who coined the term *collective unconscious* to describe the primordial and universal images that, according to Jung, have existed in the human imagination since the beginning of time. The images that make up the collective unconscious, the universal patterns and motifs that form the residue of an inborn shared human past, are called *archetypes*. Unable to discover a way to account for the recurrent images and patterns that appear in the narratives of disparate cultures, Jung suggests that archetypes, which are manifested through dreams, rituals, myths, religious beliefs, and literature, were shaped during the earliest periods of human existence. He further proposes that creative and imaginative expression derives its basic structures from natural occurrences—among them the cycle of birth and death and rebirth, the passage of seasons—or universal narrative patterns such as the *quest* or the *descent* to the *underworld*.

Archetypal critics differ in their critical methodologies, some drawing their strategies from a variety of disciplines—anthropology, history, psychology—and others relying solely on evidence from literary texts. But they do share certain core assumptions and purposes: that archetypes and archetypal patterns are universal, although they are manifested differently from culture to culture; and that the collective unconscious and its companion archetypes are the essential keys to the meaning of myth and ritual, dream and fantasy, narrative and—in the case of Amy Tan's fiction—talk story and feminine autobiography.

The Hundred Secret Senses lends itself particularly well to an archetypal analysis. To begin with, the novel contains several textual markers—narrative patterns or characters—strongly suggesting that an archetypal reading might yield valuable observations and insights. Early in the novel, Miss Banner's first attempts to speak about her life in Chinese suggest a world that defies logical comprehension—a plane of existence that normalizes little boys falling through a hole to the other side of the world, a school full of little Jesuses, money that smells like flowers and makes people happy. The description of a rationally impossible, shapeshifting world points to an archetypal universe or the dream landscape that often signals a journey into the unconscious where archetypes give shape to unarticulated thoughts. Another marker is the presence of characters who represent particular archetypes. One of these archetypal characters is Lao Lu, a *yin* person, a ghostly visitor from another existence who represents the Spirit archetype, and whose presence is a clear indicator of the tension between the novel's two worlds and the characters' multiple existences. Kwan has unfinished business from a previous life, and Lao Lu functions as her chief advisor in her efforts to complete her mission. Another archetypal figure is Big Ma whose name is a variant form of the title, "Great Mother," and who, in fact, has represented in Kwan's life the contradictory qualities of nurturance and destruction that are ascribed to the Great Mother archetype. After the death of Kwan's mother, Big Ma gave the orphaned child a home and raised her, but Kwan has always felt ambivalent about the older woman. Acknowledging Big Ma's largesse, Kwan nevertheless continues to resent the frequent slaps she endured as a child. In addition, Kwan is still bitter that Big Ma cheerfully shipped her off to America. Consequently, second only to Kwan's desire to bring Olivia and Simon back together is her need to show Big Ma that the rejected orphan has become a successful American who can afford to visit her home village bearing heaps of gifts.

Still another archetypal marker is Tan's focus on the Changmian caves. In myth and folktale, caves are privileged as significant archetypal locations, denoting primal origins, birth, and rebirth. Before Olivia and Kwan can create a satisfactory conclusion for their shared story that began a century earlier, they must travel to the caves that represent the traumatic separations of that earlier existence: en route to the caves, Nunumu sees Zeng's shadow for the last time; in those caves, Yiban faces the knowledge that he will never see Nelly Banner again; and beside those caves, Nunumu and Miss Banner are killed by the Manchu soldiers. In addition to these markers, Kwan's dream-like narratives as well as Olivia's frequent references to dreams strongly indicate an examination that derives some of its methodology and critical apparatus from dream theory, which is a significant component of archetypal criticism. One might, in fact, read *The Hundred Secret Senses* as an extended archetypal dream through which Olivia attempts to sort out the psychological confusions and uncertainties as well as the emotional chaos of her life.

Early in the novel, Olivia introduces the dream motif, saying, "Because of Kwan, I have a talent for remembering dreams," and then adding that throughout her childhood years, she believed that everyone remembered dreams as though they were other lives or even other identities. After years of drowsy listening as Kwan told stories at bedtime, and years of falling asleep while Kwan droned on at length about Changmian and *yin* people and Miss Banner, Olivia can no longer identify the boundaries between her own dreams and episodes in Kwan's stories. She is unable to recall those critical points at which her dream life seamlessly incorporated Kwan's voice spinning out events, people, and landscapes. For Olivia, dreams and stories are each part of the fabric of the other; stories are the verbal records of dreams, dreams are where the stories take shape.

The archetypal pattern that dominates *The Hundred Secret Senses* and structures the plot is the cycle of birth and death and rebirth, a pattern that is mirrored by the constant renewal in the natural world as winter gives way to spring and then summer, or the wet season succumbs to the dry months, year after year, century after century. Jungian psychologists have pointed out that the collective unconscious refuses to recognize finality, preferring instead to privilege cyclical change and renewal:

> In our dreams, as in our myths, death may figure not as the end, but as part of an overall process of growth and transformation. Just as life is born from death in the material world . . . so our psychological and spiritual energies constantly recreate themselves, assuming new forms in our imagination.

Throughout the novel, birth and death are juxtaposed, linked in ways that suggest the clear relationship between the two events in Kwan's stories as well as in the grand cycle of the universe. As a result of Jack Yee's death, Kwan is "born" into the Laguni family to become Olivia's loyal sister and friend, as well as her guide to a previous life. Years before that, Buncake must die so that Kwan can return to life, "reborn in her friend's body—again, so that eventually she can become a part of Olivia's life. And a century earlier, before Kwan's story begins, Yiban Johnson, born immediately after his mother's suicide by hanging, grows to manhood and falls in love with Nelly

Banner, only to lose her because Nunumu fails to realize how well Yiban can deduce Miss Banner's thoughts. That mistake so haunts Nunumu that her primary mission in life after she becomes Kwan is to put things right by reuniting Nelly and Yiban, who are now Olivia and Simon.

Death is a pervasive motif in *The Hundred Secret Senses*, which begins when Olivia's father dies, and ends with Big Ma's funeral and the suggestion that Kwan is dead. With the exception of Jack Yee's death from illness, the deaths in the novel are unusual, even slightly surreal, creating the ambiance of a nightmare world and underscoring the dreamlike tone of the novel. Elza dies in an avalanche that overwhelms her as she angrily skis away from Simon to whom she has just announced that she is pregnant. Big Ma is so overjoyed at Kwan's impending visit to her village that she cannot wait, and hops aboard a minibus to surprise Kwan in Guilin. En route, the bus crashes, killing Big Ma on the very day that she should have been reunited with Kwan. Years earlier, Buncake drowns while she and Kwan are ensconced in a ditch that is so dry that they are pretending to be sitting in a boat. A sudden squall produces flash floods that overwhelm the two children who drown before they can scramble to safety. Kwan's tales about Changmian in the nineteenth century include several unusual demises. When Lao Lu makes an obscene remark about General Cape and Miss Banner, a soldier (possibly Cape?) beheads him. In a bizarre scene reminiscent of mass suicide within religious cults, the missionaries end their lives rather than face torture by the Manchu soldiers. After eating stale Communion bread and drinking water that they pretend is wine, Dr. Too Late, Miss Mouse, and Pastor and Mrs. Amen pray, then together they ingest all of the pills that remain in Dr. Too Late's medicine bag. Finally, Nunumu and Miss Banner die together, just a short distance from the safety of the caves somewhere on a mountain near Changmian, possibly hanged, although Kwan discounts that possibility because she says that hanging is too much trouble to arrange in a place with no trees.

Dreams of death, whether one's own or another's, can have several interpretations. Such dreams often suggest that the dreamer is grappling with deep-seated concerns, frequently including fear of loss of self or identity, dread of retribution for some fault or sin, and fear of alienation of affection. All of these fears are personified in Olivia. Even as an adult who appears to be comfortably assimilated into American culture, Olivia is plagued with questions and doubts about her Chinese ancestry, and she steadfastly continues to resist any suggestion that she and Kwan might have far more in common than a shared father. A problematic ethnicity is not the only source of Olivia's self-doubt. For over a decade and a half, she has identified herself primarily in relation to Simon, but throughout their marriage she has been unable to let go of her belief that Simon's affection for her is inconsequential compared to the love he still feels for the long-dead Elza. Olivia is certain that for Simon she is only second-best. Coupled with her insecurities in her marriage is Olivia's recurrent guilt about her inability to accept wholeheartedly Kwan's love and loyalty, and although she has never identified what she believes the appropriate punishment might be for her emotional frigidity, her guilt is real and it creates a barrier between the two sisters. Finally, although Olivia initiated the quarrel with Simon and asked for the divorce, she is clearly unhappy with their separation. She is afraid to admit the depth of her need for Simon, and to a certain extent her sudden demand for a divorce is an extension of her fear that he might be the one who suggests that they end their marriage. During the life of their relationship, she has managed to convince herself that he does not truly value her presence in his life. Olivia is sure that for Simon she is merely a pallid substitute for Elza, and she is anxious to preempt any move he might make to dissolve the relationship.

Balancing the deaths in the novel and establishing relationships between one life and another is a series of rebirths and reincarnations that produce a sense of cyclical time and universal continuity. The Changmian–San Francisco connection is integral to the text—essential to both plot and narrative structure. In the scheme of things that Kwan has been articulating since Olivia was a child, Kwan is Nunumu in the nineteenth century story, Olivia is Miss Banner to whom Nunumu pledges her deepest loyalty, and Simon is Yiban, Miss Banner's true love. At the time of her death, Nunumu blames herself for causing the separation of Miss Banner and Yiban, and as Kwan, she is determined to do everything possible to get Olivia and Simon to Changmian where, she tells them, their fate is waiting to happen.

As has been implied, Kwan appears to be at the center of the most mystical rebirths and connections. She tells Olivia that as a child in her second life as Kwan, she drowns with her friend, Buncake. Kwan flies to the World of *Yin*, and there she meets Nelly Banner who is on the verge of returning to life as Olivia. Nelly/Olivia begs Kwan to return to life on earth so that in a few years they can be together again, and Kwan reluctantly obeys, only to discover that her body is so broken that it can no longer support life. With no other alternatives evident, she enters Buncake's unmarred body, and thereafter is her friend's doppelganger, although her mind and heart still belong to the old Kwan. This incident, minor though it appears to be in the almost epic story of Kwan and Olivia, highlights the durability and longevity of the emotional bonds that exist between them, and illustrates the cyclical patterns that inform and undergird the fictional universe of *The Hundred Secret Senses*.

The cycle of death and rebirth is echoed in the legend of Changmian, the village that serves as the setting for Kwan's narratives in two centuries. In

Kwan's version of the legend, when the Manchu soldiers ravaged the countryside in the war against the Taiping, Changmian's villagers fled to the nearby caves in the mountains where they concealed themselves. Failing to induce the villagers to come out of their refuges, the soldiers built huge bonfires at the cave entrances, but succeeded only in smoking out thousands of bats whose frantically flapping wings fanned the flames, turning the entire valley, including Changmian, into an inferno. Only two or three soldiers escaped the conflagration, and relief troops who arrived a week later found nothing but a completely, eerily, empty village and hundreds of new graves. But one month later, according to Kwan, a traveler passing Changmian found a thriving village full of people and dogs, all carrying on with their daily activities as though they had been doing so week after week without interruption. To compound the traveler's bafflement and unease, the village people claimed never to have seen any soldiers. Not surprisingly, once the traveler left the valley and recounted his strange experience, Changmian acquired a reputation for being a "village of ghosts."

When Olivia and Simon see Changmian for the first time, they notice immediately that the village appears completely untouched by time. Changmian's name, which has two possible and opposite meanings, emphasizes the village's timeless and somewhat unearthly appearance, and foregrounds the contradictions in its history. Kwan tells Olivia and Simon that the word *chang* means "sing" while *mian* suggests "silk," with the combination indicating "something soft but go on forever like thread" or a never-ending quiet melody. She adds, however, that it is also possible to pronounce Changmian differently, thus producing a contrasting meaning in which *chang* means "long" and *mian* indicates "sleep," creating the phrase "long sleep," which is a synonym for death. Embedded in those two meanings are death and rebirth—the juxtaposition of long sleep with the idea of a soft melody that never ends—the two constants in Kwan's stories and, it seems, in the relationship between Kwan and Olivia, and between Olivia and Simon. The rebirth of Changmian, as well as that village's implied participation as the site of Kwan's own cycle of birth and death and rebirth, makes the village the ideal place for Olivia's own reconnection with herself. Her story begins in Changmian and is interrupted there, and she must return not just to the village but also to the nearby caves to complete and continue the cycle that is her life.

In *The Secret Language of Dreams*, British psychologist David Fontana points out that archetypal dreams tend to occur at major transitional points in life, or during periods of uncertainty and disruption. He adds further that such dreams "mark the process toward individuation and spiritual maturity." Olivia is in the midst of an emotionally and psychologically disruptive transitional point in her life—the break-up of her marriage to the man whom she has loved more than anyone else in her entire life. It is no consolation to Olivia to recall that she has precipitated the separation from Simon; her emotional pain is genuine and devastating. Kwan is likewise at a major transitional point: her fiftieth birthday, which is a milestone that marks half a century of life. Together, Olivia and Kwan embark on their shared archetypal quest, the journey to discover wholeness and integration. Significantly, they travel to a foreign country, an action that in archetypal dreams suggests a journey into the unconscious in search of wholeness; and their travel to China takes them to the east, toward a compass point that suggests rebirth and rejuvenation. They are leaving behind them their San Francisco past, moving toward the landscape of an older shared past, to put their lives in order for the future, which is linked to their shared histories. At the end of the quest, in China, Olivia and Kwan are finally able to rediscover and to assimilate the scattered fragments of their lives and their identities: Kwan is reconciled with Big Ma; Olivia and Simon reconnect; and Olivia acknowledges not just the existence but also the strength and permanence of the bond between herself and Kwan.

Salvation comes to the sisters in different ways. For Kwan, it is the opportunity finally to articulate to Olivia the still-unvoiced remainder of their shared history, to confess the guilt that has burdened her from one lifetime to another because she told the lie that makes her responsible for inadvertently separating Nelly Banner and Yiban Johnson. When she concludes her story on the rainy mountainside near Changmian, she is noticeably relieved. "Now you know all my secret," she tells Olivia. "Give me peace." Her final words are reassurances that Simon loves Olivia, and that Olivia has never been a substitute for Elza. And with that, Kwan enters the secret cave and disappears from Olivia's life. During the week-long search for Kwan, Olivia commences her own journey toward an integrated self as she and Simon slowly begin to reexplore their relationship. Her discovery of the eggs in the Ghost Merchant's garden suggests that new possibilities await her, that her life might change in ways that she has not anticipated.

The novel ends with the final juxtaposition of death and rebirth. Early on the morning of Kwan's disappearance, Simon and Olivia make love for the first time in months on a bed that has belonged to Kwan's family for generations. Nine months later, Olivia gives birth to Samantha, and as Samantha grows into toddlerhood, her favorite toy is the music box that Kwan gave Olivia for a wedding gift. Olivia no longer has Kwan, but in her sister's place is little Samantha whose presence has created a new relationship between her parents. Olivia and Simon have begun to try to resolve their differences, to learn to communicate openly and without rancor, to enjoy being together—with Samantha—as a family. Out of Kwan's death has come life and the strengthening of emotional bonds. And at last, Olivia knows that "the world is not a place but the vastness of the soul. And the soul is nothing more than love, limitless, endless."

YUAN YUAN

The Semiotics of China Narratives in the Con/texts of Kingston and Tan

"How 'Chinese' is *The Woman Warrior*?" Sau-ling Cynthia Wong asks in her essay "Kingston's Handling of Traditional Chinese Sources." The native-ness of ethnic American literature is a complex issue that deserves serious consideration and intelligent discussion. I have noticed that to date it is not the nativeness of our ethnic narratives that has escaped critical attention but the narrative reconfiguration of nativeness in literary representation. That is to say, the whole issue of nativeness in literary texts requires careful examination in the context of cultural differences and in relation to subject positions. In this essay, I explore the theoretical implications of that "native" issue by inquiring into the semiotics of "China experiences" in terms of "China narratives" within the contexts of Maxine Hong Kingston's *The Woman Warrior* and *China Men* and Amy Tan's *The Joy Luck Club* and *The Kitchen God's Wife*.

The "China experiences" presented by Kingston and Tan emerge as narratives of recollection—which means that in their novels they have reconstructed various narratives of experiences in China against the background of American society and within the context of American culture. Their China narratives emerge in the "other" cultural context informed by a complex process of translation, translocation, and transfiguration of the original experiences in China. In fact, China experiences are generally

From *Critique* Vol. 40, No. 3 (Spring 1999). © 1999 by the Society for the Study of Multi-Ethnic Literature of the U.S.

transfigured into "China narratives" only after they have lost their reference to China; thus they are related more to the present American situation than to their original context in Chinese society. The present American context provides meaning and determines the content of the China narrative. Only under such circumstances as loss of origin can China experiences emerge as a China narrative—a text reconfigured within other contexts. "China narrative," therefore, differs from China experiences and signifies a specific kind of self-reflexive discourse that is reinscribed within another cultural context to serve specific purposes: self-affirmation or self-negation, remembrance or repression. Eventually, in the novels of both Kingston and Tan, China as a geographical location is transliterated into a semiotic space of recollection; China as personal experiences is translated into a cultural repository for reproduction; and, as a text, China is reconfigured into a variety of discourses: myth, legend, history, fantasy, films, and talk-stories.

The China narrative in both Kingston and Tan serves as an undercurrent but central text that structures the present relationship between mothers and daughters because of the specific position it occupies in their lives. Therefore, the cross-cultural hermeneutics of China is conducted within that domestic space, between two generations in general and between the Chinese mothers and their American-born daughters in specific. As products of different cultures and histories, mothers and daughters abide by different cultural values and possess different modes of interpretation. In fact, they speak entirely different languages whenever they talk about China. "My mother and I spoke two different languages, which we did," Jing-Mei Woo says in *The Joy Luck Club*, "I talked to her in English, she answered back in Chinese." The bilingual conversation turns into a game of translation; and in that translation, meaning is transfigured, displaced, and occasionally, lost. As Jing-Mei Woo says: "We translated each other's meanings and I seemed to hear less than what was said, while my mother heard more."

Both mothers and daughters constantly have to re-evaluate their respective China narratives that are grounded in entirely different cultural contexts, with different historical references and subject positions. For the mothers, China narratives inform a process of recollection (history or loss of it) whereas for the daughters, who have never been there, China narratives become a text of culture. In other words, China experiences as semiotic texts are reconstituted through a choice of two modes of discourse: history or culture. Eventually, China becomes a semiotic site where culture and identity are fought over, negotiated, displaced, and transformed. Instead of being a static ontological presence of a uitary category, China becomes a hermeneutic space for articulating identity and difference, a process that governs the cultural and historical reconstitution of the subjects.

MOTHER'S LOSS NARRATIVE:
RECOLLECTING AND REPOSITIONING

In Tan's *The Joy Luck Club* and *The Kitchen God's Wife*, loss functions as the dominant metaphor for the mothers' China narratives and the central code to decipher their existence. Each mother's story of her China experiences eventually develops into a semiotics of loss. Hence, moving to America means to them loss of identity and the reality of existence—being reduced to ghosts in alien territory. Even though mothers and daughters interpret China with different codes and from different positions, they are all overshadowed by a prevalent sense of loss. To quote Ying-Ying St. Clair in *The Joy Luck Club*: "We are lost." The daughters seem to be lost between cultures whereas the mothers appear to have lost everything. Later in the same novel, Jing-Mei Woo says of her mother: "She had come here in 1949 after losing everything in China: her mother and father, her family home, her first husband, and two daughters, twin baby girls."

In *The Kitchen God's Wife*, the China narrative is based on Winnie's painful experiences in China. In fact, the pain and suffering that are central to Winnie's recollection invite repression rather than recall. Her China narrative is subject to constant postponement and erasure to conceal the unspeakable experience and repressed memory. As Winnie says: "Now I can forget my tragedies, put all my secrets behind a door that will never be opened, never seen by American eyes." Memory for Winnie embodies loss or pain; her China narrative essentially requires concealing instead of unfolding Remembering inevitably entails pain and, eventually, desire for repression transforms into a necessity of repression. Winnie's experience of China is transfigured into a discourse of repression and her recollection of China experiences is translated into a loss narrative.

Within the American context, mothers' recollections of China experiences demonstrate more loss of memory than recall of the past. Forgetting, paradoxically, becomes the key to recollection. In *The Joy Luck Club*, Jing-Mei Woo complained of her mother's repeating the same Kweilin story to her in various versions. She said: "I never thought my mother's Kweilin story was anything but a Chinese fairy tale. The endings always changed.[. . .] The story always grew and grew." In *The Kitchen God's Wife*, Winnie, failing to recall her mother, provides us contradictory versions of her mother's image, believing her to be pretty, strong, educated, and coming from a good family. But later she admits that "maybe my mother was not pretty at all, and I only want to believe that she was." That is why Winnie keeps repeating to herself: "Now I no longer know which story is the truth, what was the real reason why she left. They are all the same, all true, all false. So much pain in everyone. I tried to tell myself, The past is gone, nothing to be done, just forget it. That's what I tried to believe." Because of memory loss, there is simply no prior text present to initiate recollection in the first place. Hence, recollection radically alters itself in a creative process. "Loss narrative" becomes the central feature that characterizes the mother's China narrative. In short, China lies at an absolute distance from present remembrance, irretrievably lost beyond recall, made present only through a narrative that invites forgetting instead of remembering.

Ironically, China, lost or otherwise, functions as the locus that defines the mother's sense of reality. American experience, on the other hand, only characterizes her marginal existence and alien position. Mothers tend to have their home and identity centered elsewhere—in China. In *The Woman Warrior*, Kingston writes: "Whenever my parents said 'home,' they suspended America." Life in America, for her mother, is too disappointing to be real. The China experience, at least, can be transliterated into a body of ideas and vocabulary that gives her a unique sense of reality and presence. Hence, China narrative, which is both defining and defined by the mothers, becomes an imaginary text of China with a displaced mentality and exile consciousness, conditioned by both repression and nostalgia.

Therefore, recollection reveals a process of negotiation with the past, constantly translating and revising the past into a narrative that grants reality to present situations. In a displaced context, the mothers have constructed China narratives for themselves and for each other. One mother, Helen, who figures in *The Kitchen God's Wife*, comments on the past to Winnie: "She and I have changed the past many times, for many reasons. And sometimes she changes it for me and does not even know what she has done." It is indeed ironical that at the end of the novel both of them are compelled to tell truths that they no longer remember, and continue to recount them only after they have lost memory. That is why Pearl, Winnie's daughter, complains: "I am laughing, confused, caught in endless circles of lies." The past, paradoxically, is lost in the process of recollection.

China is, so to speak, a "mother land," a repository of history with haunting memories and extraordinary experiences—a repository for reproduction. The mothers constantly revise their China narratives in terms of their present conscious needs and unconscious desires, asserting them in the context of American culture for self-empowerment.

China experiences, or the past in general, even though forgotten to a certain extent, have always been reconstituted by the mothers into narratives that carry out special missions: to control the fate of their "American-made" daughters. Thus, the loss narrative is transformed into an authoritative discourse. In *The Kitchen God's Wife*, Winnie says to her daughter: "In China back then, you were always responsible to somebody else. It's not like here in the United States—freedom, independence, individual thinking, do what you want, disobey your mother. No such thing." In that case, she has transformed an absent text into a powerful narrative for the purpose of domination. She is using China narrative to establish and reinforce her present authoritative position in America.

Lacking ontological stability and lost in constant recollection, China narrative is fabricated and manipulated in various forms. Ironically, the power of China narrative resides precisely in its "loss of reality." In *The Joy Luck Club*, the mothers, who assume the absolute authority on China, transform China into a semiotic space wherein they can continue to exercise the power that they have lost in the other context—the Chinese society. Collectively, they have constructed another cultural territory, actually an extra-territory within American society. Eventually, China experiences in the mothers' narratives are translated into a mode of discourse, a style of domineering, a tongue for control, and a gesture for having authority over the daughters' lives and molding their subjectivity. In that case, China becomes less a geographical location than a cultural extra-territory that the mothers have created in order to construct the subjectivity of their "American-made" daughters.

China experiences become a repository of potential power from which the mothers draw excessive narratives that support their exercise of control. Sometimes, they turn their China experiences into a disciplinary lesson that reinforces restrictive cultural values (Brave Orchid's story of the dead aunt); sometimes they translate their personal memory into a fantastic tale with powerful seduction (Suyun Woo's Kweilin story); and sometimes they transliterate China into a secret text from which daughters are excluded and only the mothers themselves have direct access (Winnie's story). As Lena St. Clair in *The Joy Luck Club* says: "When we were alone, my mother would speak in Chinese, saying things my father could not possibly imagine. I could understand the words perfectly, but not the meaning." That is, only the mother possesses the key to decode the meaning of China narrative. Hence, Chinese, a secondary language to the daughters, becomes the mothers' primary discourse strategy to manipulate their daughters. The mother in *The Joy Luck Club*, reminds her daughter that because *The Book of Twenty-Six Malignant Gates* is written in Chinese "You cannot understand it. That is why you must listen to me." Daughters, on the other hand, resist their mothers' China narratives by reminding them that their stories are out of the context because, as Jing-Mei Woo asserts, "this wasn't China."

In *The Joy Luck Club*, Jing-Mei Woo says of her mother: "Over the years, she told me the same story, except for the ending, which grew darker, casting long shadows into her life, and eventually into mine." Apparently, the mothers are using their narrative powers to construct their daughter's identities, as if to continue the "remarkable" China experiences and to extend Chinese history and culture through their daughters' existence. Although transfigured into authoritative discourses that dominate the daughters, China narratives are in effect grounded on the semiotics of loss. Hence, China narrative is but a ghost story: an absence resides at the very center of the text that determines its ultimate signification.

DAUGHTER'S TRANSLATION:
FATHER'S SILENCE AND MOTHER'S TALK-STORIES

In Kingston's *The Woman Warrior* and *China Men*, the daughter's experience of China as a semiotic space is structured in a polarized position between her mother's complicated talk-stories on the one hand and her father's impenetrable silence on the other. That intertextual relationship between presence and absence determines the semiotic function of China narrative for Kingston. She has to decode her father's silence and her mother's speech, a process involving more than simply attempting to locate her mother in *The Woman Warrior* or seeking her father in *China Men*. In both novels, Kingston finds herself by negotiating her relation to her parents, to a semiotic space defined as China narrative, and to the Chinese culture.

Kingston's *China Men* is composed against the background of her father's silence. Kingston writes to her father: "You say with the few words and the silences: No Stories. No past. No China." For her, China is a country she made up within an American context, along with her history and her family mythology in *China Men*. She dramatizes her ancestors' memory in a grand style by transliterating the "oral history" into a cultural epic.

As a daughter, Kingston feels both compelled and obligated to speak on her father's behalf, to decipher his silence of the past, to hear his China narrative. Kingston writes: "You kept up a silence for weeks and months. We invented the terrible things you were thinking." Similarly, she invents a China narrative for her father and writes into American history the contributions of the Chinese laborers by reconstructing a legendary text for the "people without history." Kingston writes: "I'll tell you what I suppose from your silences and few words, and you can tell me that I'm mistaken. You just have to speak up with the real stories if I've got you wrong." She wants to know "the Chinese stories"; she wants to go back to China to see her "ancestral village"; and she wants to meet "the people with fabulous imaginations." Kingston writes: "I want to discern what it is that makes people go West and turn into Americans. I want to compare China, a country I made up, with what country is really out there."

Thus, in *China Men*, Kingston formulates father land or China in an imaginary space wherein she offered various versions of her father's origin. However, root-seeking always ends up elsewhere. She has to speak truth by creating legends, making a legendary history for her father, reconstructing a China narrative for him in his absence. In short, she creates myth out of silence and legend out of absence. The China narrative in *China Men* is entirely created by the daughter who dedicates a history to the father.

In *The Woman Warrior*, Kingston is asking: "Chinese-American, when you try to understand what things in you are Chinese, how do you separate what is peculiar to childhood, to poverty, insanities, one family, your mother who marked your growing with stories, from what is Chinese? What is Chinese tradition and what is the movies?" Kingston confronts the perplexing issue of China narrative within the context of her mother's talk-stories and her own fantasy, forbidden tales and her own dreams. About "a great power, my mother talking-story," Kingston observes: "I couldn't tell where the stories left off and the dreams began, her voice and the voice of the heroines in my sleep." "Real" China seems to lie at the distance of the inevitable loss.

China narrative in *The Woman Warrior* is, first of all, translated from personal experience into a narrative of recollection. Her mother's China narrative, based on the recollection of her direct experience of China, is transfigured into a "historical" text. That text is further reconfigured in the American context into her daughter's bicultural text that consists of recapitulation of her mother's talk-stories. Evidently, Kingston's knowledge of China is based on her (m)other's narratives and, eventually, Kingston's China narrative becomes a translation of a translation—in fact, a cultural reconstruction. That accounts for Kingston's reconstitution of her dead aunt's sexual identity according to Western code and American culture. In that instance, historical and cultural reconstruction of China is divided along bicultural views and bifocal perspectives.

The daughter's China narrative, based on the primary text of her mother's recollection, by way of myths, legends, talk-stories, informs the operation of a second order linguistic system. That is to say, the daughter's cognition of China seems always to be structured, mediated, and overdetermined by the semiotics of the (m)other tongue that serves as the first order symbolic signification. Therefore, the daughter's reconstruction of the China narrative is based on the signifier of the first linguistic order (her mother's narrative) that assumes a historical reference to China. The mother's narrative functions as the ultimate interpretative frame of the daughter's reconceptualization of China, actually, the absolute horizon of the daughter's cognition of China. Put more precisely, her mother's China narrative itself constitutes the absolute horizon of Kingston's recognition of China experiences.

In her mother's talk-stories, China resides in a domain of memory based on personal experience of social reality. For Kingston, China is a territory of dream and fantasy. In her dreams, she has revenged her family, fantasizing her China experiences as compensation for "disappointing American life." But, of course, those China experiences are entirely based on the tales of and from China by way of her mother's talk-stories that have already been translated in a new cultural context and with reference to their American experiences. In *Boundaries of the Self: Gender, Culture, Fiction,* Roberta Rubenstein points out: "Their offspring born in America inherit this split between cultures without ever having seen their ancestral land, except imaginatively, through their elders' eyes." And this is exactly Kingston's vision—filtered through her mother's eyes and her mother's tongue. Her mother's stories radically shape her vision of China and the Chinese—the place of her ancestral origin. From that displaced context and removed memory, she invents a China in a fantasy space, reconfiguring the ghost of China to inscribe her present subject position. Growing up in America, she has to distinguish what is supernatural and what is real, what are ghosts and what are people.

INDIVIDUATION FROM THE (M)OTHER: GHOST OR OTHERWISE

In Kingston's *The Woman Warrior*, the boundaries between self and the other are not clearly defined until the daughter confronts and reinscribes the past, the China experience. The daughter is forced to negotiate her position between conflicting sets of discourses: of family, ethnicity, culture, history, and nationality. To reach a reconciliation, Kingston must come to terms with herself in relation to the historical situation she inherits from her mother and then must choose her own subject position. She has to extricate herself from the identity fabricated by her mother's China narrative and assert her own subject position by reconfiguring bicultural discourse.

Both mother and daughter develop multiple discourses to encode their existences. Both attempt to carve out a personal space in an alien culture that has limited and marginalized their lives, their heritage, and their language. Kingston, however, living on the edges of two communities, has to choose between her mother's home culture and the alien culture. *The Woman Warrior* dramatizes Kingston's growing up among contradictions and confusions between cultures and languages. Wendy Ho remarks: "Like her mother, the daughter negotiates the preservation and the subversion of aspects of traditional Chinese culture against the pressures of the mainstream of Western society. However, she is in a precarious position of her own: she is not Chinese enough for her mother, father and ethnic community and not American-feminine enough to find a home among the white 'ghost'."

Kingston writes: "They would not tell us children because we had been born among ghosts, were taught by ghosts, and were ourselves ghost-like. They called us a kind of ghosts." Ghost represents tension and problems of language and cultural system. However, Kingston refuses to be reduced to simply a ghost in "an alien culture." Instead, she positively recreates a unique identity separate from the ghost position. In *The Woman Warrior*, she has to confront all the ghosts from China with which her mother has haunted her childhood: Fa Mu La, her mother Brave Orchid, the dead aunt, Moon Orchid, and herself. She has to transcend that ghost terrain to enter "a ghost-free country."

Ghosts in her narrative possess multiple perspectives. They are signifiers with diverse meanings, especially when configured in a multicultural context. In "*The Woman Warrior* as a Search for Ghost," Gayle K. Fujita Sato remarks: "'Ghosts' define two antithetical worlds that threaten the narrator's sense of a unified self. How is she to articulate her own location, which is 'Chinese American,' when history, tradition, and family have formulated 'China' and 'America' as reciprocally alien territories?"

Kingston refuses to live a hyphenated experience and remain a victim to her mother's China narrative. She manages to go beyond her mother's talk-stories by subverting the designated position defined by her mother's past experience. Self-production depends upon both preservation and progression. On the one hand, by resisting her mother's codification of her identity as a Chinese slave-girl, Kingston disrupts the "slave narrative"; on the other hand, she rejects the ex-centric self, discontent with being reduced to an unnamable ghost in an alien culture. In effect, Kingston transcends the boundaries of both cultures by rewriting the China narrative once authorized by her mother and rejecting the displaced China experience in American society.

In *The Woman Warrior*, Kingston is refuting not simply China, Chinese culture, or the (m)other tongue, but the "Chineseness" that is specifically produced under the new historical and cultural circumstances. She resists the victimization of stereotypification by establishing a separate identity aside from the "Chineseness" forged in America—the artificial construct of the Chinese that diminishes her status and delimits her power. Therefore, her separation from the mother signifies the process of individuation from both mother's land and mother's tongue and results in her finding her own reality and space in existence and creating her own language and authority. Kingston is determined that she has to "leave home to see the world logically." She says: "I continue to sort out what's just my childhood, just my imagination, just my family, just the village, just movies, just living. [. . .] Soon I want to go to China and find out who's lying [. . .]."

TRANSLATING THE IN-BETWEEN POSITION: RE-CREATION

Each ethnic group constructs a unique self-image that reflects its response to the impact of the dominant culture. Their reactions vary according to their different positions, to the social environments, and to the dominant value systems. The self that emerges can be defensive, aiming to preserve the original cultural values and keeping its alienation and marginality. Or the self can be extensive, losing marginality by mediating between two cultures. Thus, multicultural environments force each ethnic group to balance a duality and negotiate the distance.

In *The Woman Warrior*, Kingston is both part of and apart from the two separate worlds; she positions herself across languages and across cultures. The double perspective of the home culture and the other culture can be both disabling and enabling, delimiting and empowering. I would argue that the self, instead of dangling as a double-alienated outsider, can succeed in bridging the two cultures and merging the duality.

The in-between situation, I believe, does not necessarily inform a split duality of inherent contradiction. It signifies not so much a fissure as a bridge that both divides and connects. Kingston acknowledges the influence of both cultures that exist not as an antithesis that excludes each other but as an integration that combines both. She is at home in this duality. She does not want to build a wall that divides but to create a bridge that connects.

For instance, Kingston does not simply question the traditional mythology of China but also incorporates it into her writing. Thus she revives part, the useful part, of the mythology instead of repressing it. Kingston appropriates Fa Mu Lan by configuring it into a new cultural context. Thus it emerges as a paradox: She uses the power of Chinese mythology to reinforce her American identity, thereby transcending the customary ways of defining the self and defying the village mentality of Chinatown. In this case, ethnicity no longer hampers her ways of thinking but enriches her imagination, which is feasting on diverse traditions and cultures.

I would argue that this in-between position, instead of producing a "feeling of being between worlds, totally at home nowhere," is not inherently a negative one. It can be positively employed. Kingston's novels demonstrate the phenomenon of multicultural texts. In *The Woman Warrior*, Kingston says: "I learned to make my mind large, as the universe is large, so that there is room for paradoxes." That is why Kingston asks her mother: "Does it make sense to you that if we're no longer attached to one piece of land, we belong to the planet?" Evidently, she creates a paradoxical self in *The Woman Warrior* that reflects the diversity of American culture.

I entirely agree with what Amy Ling says in *Between Worlds: Woman Writers of Chinese Ancestry* about the second generation immigrant experiences:

> The very condition [of the between-world] itself carries both negative and positive charges. On the one hand, being between worlds can be interpreted to mean occupying the space or gulf between two banks; one is thus in a state of suspension, accepted by neither side and therefore truly belonging nowhere.[. . .] On the other hand, viewed from a different perspective, being between worlds may be considered as having footholds on both banks and therefore belonging to two worlds at once. One does not have less; one has more [. . .], the person between worlds is in the indispensable position of being a bridge.

Kingston's use of China narrative transcends its original contexts. Her translocation of Chinese mythology signifies cultural replacement and re-position that help her form a distinctive identity of her own. She creates her own mythology within the myth of Fa Mu Lan. That paradoxical borrowing emerges as a border issue of bridging instead of separating. She has to separate herself from her ancestral village and its traditions and enter the complex multicultural reality of her American experiences. Paradoxically, her fantasy of China has saved her from a totally depressing fate in America. The Chinese mythology functions as a semiotic empowerment in the process of identity formation.

Moreover, what is the American identity if not paradoxical? Historically, American identity has always been defined in relation to the other: other places, other cultures, and other times. That double perspective is a uniquely American phenomenon. In fact, Kingston's perplexity over identity touches on an issue essential to American culture. Hence, her search for identity reveals those complex cultural transactions: her American identity is reinforced by Chinese mythology that, even though somewhat relegated to the "other" category, nevertheless functions as the ideological basis of her self construction. She is not simply repeating what has been taught to her, but is adapting Chinese mythology to her present situation with an imaginative creativity. Still, as Sau-Ling Cynthia Wong allows: "Whether her alterations to traditional material constitute creative adaptation or willful exploitation, realistic reflection or second-generation cultural disorientation or irresponsible perversion of a precious heritage, is a question teachers must work through with their students."

Robert G. Lee also agrees that "for Kingston, myths, necessarily rebuilt, have a strategic value in helping to analyze contemporary events. She recognizes that the power of myth resides in its capacity to be recontextualized and inscribed with new meanings." Apparently, the new historical circumstances may actually require that Kingston refabricate the mythical texture of her narrative. She herself argues in her essay "Cultural Mis-Readings by American Reviewers" that the Chinese mythology in *The Woman Warrior* is "but one transformed by America." She reminds us again of what many people fail to recognize: that the "Chinese myths have been transmuted by America." She observes in her "Personal Statement" that myths and lives maintain a dialogic interrelation and "the myths transform lives and are themselves changed." "Sinologists have criticized me for not knowing myths and for distorting them. [. . .] They don't understand that myths have to change, be useful or be forgotten. Like the people who carry them across oceans, the myths become American. The Myths I write are new, American." Instead of being controlled by Chinese mythology, Kingston rewrites it to create her own American myth.

In "'Emerging Canons' of Asian American Literature and Art," Amy Ling asks: "Must the multicultural writer/artist be totally and exclusively answerable to his or her ethnic community, be the spokesperson of that community, tell the community's stories and tell them accurately? Or can she or he claim the right to express an individual vision and personal concerns, and to modify the myths and legends of a group to his or her own artistic purpose?" I believe that that question involves the issue of subject position for both Kingston and Tan. That is, who is writing, a Chinese or an American?

Writing, for Kingston and Tan, means a process of confrontation, discovery, and creation of their cultural identities. Both present themselves as American novelists of Chinese descent, resisting the hyphenated experience embodied by the so-called "mestiza consciousness." Accordingly, their novels represent American people and contribute to American literature. Therefore, their writings mark a transition from the position of separation and alienation to that of accommodation and re-position, initiating a positive self-invention instead of a denial of ethnic origin. Apparently, they go beyond mere justification of ethnic identity but are related to the issue of re-creation and re-placement. The creative negotiation between self and the other can effectively reinforce the ethnic subject—the assertion of the repressed subject within a multicultural context.

Both Kingston and Tan write to reconstitute the American experience through the strategy of difference, highlighting the importance of difference within American cultures by challenging the status quo of American identity.

Both argue for participating in cultural construction instead of remaining in a stereotypical position as temporary sojourners—alienated and displaced personalities. I believe that gesture challenges the very constitution of the Americanness of American culture and identity.

In an interview with Paula Rabinowitz, Kingston remarked: "Actually, I think my books are much more American than they are Chinese. I felt that I was building, creating, myself and these people as American people, to make everyone realize that they are American people. [. . .] Also, I am creating part of American literature, and I was very aware of doing that, of adding to American literature." In "Cultural Mis-Readings by American Reviewers," she reasserts her position as an American writer: "I am an American. I am an American writer, who, like other American writers, wants to write the great American novel. *The Woman Warrior* is an American book." Interestingly enough, the issue of China narrative in the novels of Kingston and Tan ends up somewhere in American literature.

Chronology

1952   Amy Ruth Tan born on February 19, in Oakland, California, to John Yueh-han, a Baptist minister and Beijing-educated electrical engineer, and Daisy (Tu Ching) Tan, a vocational nurse and member of a Joy Luck Club whose stories about her life in China have been an inspiration in many of Tan's works; she has recently been diagnosed with Alzheimer's disease.

1960   First published work, "What the Library Means to Me," appears in the Santa Rosa *Press Democrat*.

1967   Tan's older brother, Peter, dies of a brain tumor; seven months later, her father dies of a brain tumor; shortly afterward, doctors discover that her mother has a benign brain tumor. Mother confesses that she had been married to an abusive man in China and has three daughters whom she lost track of after the Communists came to power. After deaths of brother and father, mother takes Amy and her younger brother, John, Jr., to live in Switzerland.

1970   Mother sends Amy to Baptist college in Oregon; Amy defies her, abandons pre-med studies to pursue study of English and linguistics; follows her boyfriend to San Jose City College.

1973   Receives a B.A. in English and linguistics from San Jose State University. Jobs include bartender, switchboard operator, carhop, horoscope writer, and pizza maker.

1974   Receives an M.A. from San Jose State University; marries the boyfriend, Louis M. DeMattei, a tax attorney, on April 6.

1974–76   Enrolled in doctoral program at University of California, Santa Cruz, and later, at Berkeley, through 1976. Leaves doctoral studies to pursue interest in working with the developmentally disabled as a language development consultant to the Alameda County Association for Retarded Citizens.

1976–81   Language consultant to programs for disabled children, Alameda County Association for Mentally Retarded, Oakland.

1980–81   Project director, MORE Project, San Francisco. Freelance business writer for IBM, Apple, and AT&T.

1981–83   Reporter, managing editor, and associate publisher for *Emergency Room Reports*.

1985   Short story, "Endgame," published in *Seventeen* magazine. Publishing agent asks her to write a book outline.

1983–87   Freelance technical writer; begins writing fiction and taking jazz piano lessons as a form of therapy to engage her "workaholic" energies. In 1987, Tan accompanies her mother to China for a reunion with the three other daughters. Publishing agent asks her to write a book from the 1985 outline. Tan quits business writing to finish the work, completed in four months, which becomes *The Joy Luck Club*.

1989   *The Joy Luck Club* published; receives Commonwealth Club gold award for fiction, Bay Area Book Reviewers award for best fiction, American Library Association's best book for young adults award, nomination for National Book Critics Circle award for best novel, and nomination for *Los Angeles Times* book award; on *New York Times* bestseller list for eight months. A short story, "Two Kinds," published in *Atlantic*.

1990   Critical essays "The Language of Discretion" and "Mother Tongue" published.

1991   *The Kitchen God's Wife* published; designated 1991 Booklist editor's choice and nominated for Bay Area Book Reviewers award. Receives Best American Essays award; awarded honorary LHD, Dominican College. A short story, "Peanut's Fortune," published in *Grand Street*.

1992   *The Moon Lady*, a children's book, published (illustrated by Gretchen Schields).

1993   Writes screenplay, with Ronald Bass, for *The Joy Luck Club*.

1994   *The Siamese Cat*, a children's book, published (illustrated by Gretchen Schields).

1995   Novels, *The Hundred Secret Senses* and *The Year of No Flood* published.

2001   *The Bonesetter's Daughter* is published.

Amy Tan lives in San Francisco and New York City.

Contributors

HAROLD BLOOM is Sterling Professor of the Humanities at Yale University and Henry W. and Albert A. Berg Professor of English at the New York University Graduate School. He is the author of over 20 books, including *The Anxiety of Influence* (1973), which sets forth Professor Bloom's provocative theory of the literary relationships between the great writers and their predecessors. His most recent book, *Shakespeare: The Invention of the Human* (1998), was a finalist for the 1998 National Book Award. Professor Bloom is a 1985 MacArthur Foundation Award recipient, served as the Charles Eliot Norton Professor of Poetry at Harvard University in 1987–88, and has received honorary degrees from the universities of Rome and Bologna. In 1999, Professor Bloom received the prestigious American Academy of Arts and Letters Gold Medal for Criticism.

MALINI JOHAR SCHUELLER is associate professor of American literature at the University of Florida. She is the author of *The Politics of Voice: Liberalism and Social Criticism from Franklin to Kingston*, as well as many essays on ethnic American writers and on the subject of imperialism in American literature.

Before his retirement in 1996, WALTER SHEAR was a professor of English at Pittsburg State University in Kansas for more than 30 years.

MARINA HEUNG teaches film and literature in the Department of English at Baruch College, CUNY.

BEN XU is the author of *Situational Tensions of Critic-Intellectuals: Thinking Through Literary Politics with Edward Said and Frank Lentricchia.*

STEPHEN SOURIS is Assistant Professor of English at Texas Women's University. He is the author of articles on Marcel Proust and Kaye Gibbons.

VICTORIA CHEN is Assistant Professor of Communication at Denison University. She has contributed several book chapters and her work has appeared in *Research on Language and Social Interaction, International and Intercultural Communication Annual.* She is co-editor of *Our Voices: Essays in Culture, Ethnicity, and Communication.*

WENDY HO is assistant professor of Asian American Studies and Women's Studies at the University of California, Davis.

E. D. HUNTLEY is Professor of English and Associate Dean of Graduate Studies at Appalachian State University. She is the author of *V.C. Andrews: A Critical Companion* and is completing a two-volume anthology of Native American plays, the critical volume *First Nations: A Research Guide to Native American Drama*, and a study of the works of Maxine Hong Kingston.

YUAN YUAN is Associate Professor of Literature and Writing at California State University in San Marcos, California.

Bibliography

Angier, Carole. "*The Joy Luck Club,*" *New Statesman & Society* (30 June 1989): 35.

Baker, John F., and Calvin Reid. "Fresh Voices, New Audiences," *Publisher's Weekly* (9 August 1993): 32.

Beard, Carla. Amy Tan's *The Joy Luck Club.* Piscataway, NJ: Research and Education Association, 1996.

Bellafonte, Gina. "People," *Time* (14 September 1992): 79.

Braendlin, Bonnie. "Mother/Daughter Dialog(ic)s In, Around, and About Amy Tan's *The Joy Luck Club,*" *Private Voices, Public Lives: Women Speak on the Literary Life.* Ed. Nancy Owen Nelson. Denton: University of North Texas Press, 1995.

Caesar, Judith. "Patriarchy, Imperialism, and Knowledge in *The Kitchen God's Wife,*" *North Dakota Quarterly,* 62, no. 4 (Fall 1994): 164–74.

Colker, David. "Learn a Little of Her Story," *Los Angeles Times* (22 December 1995): E3.

Davis, Rocio G. "Wisdom (Un)heeded: Chinese Mothers and American Daughters in Amy Tan's *The Joy Luck Club,*" *Cuadernos de Investigacion Filologica* 19–20 (1993–94): 89–100.

Dew, Rob Forman. "*The Kitchen God's Wife,*" *New York Times Book Review* (16 June, 1991): 9.

Drolet, Anne McCart. *Telling Her Stories to Change the Con(text) of Identity: Four Novels by Contemporary American Women Authors of Color. DAI* 54, no. 8 (February 1994): 9402954.

Duke, Michael. "Red Ivy, and Green Earth Mother," *World Literature Today* 65, no. 2 (Spring 1991): 361.

Feldman, Gayle. "*The Joy Luck Club:* Chinese Magic, American Blessings, and a Publishing Fairy Tale," *Publisher's Weekly* (7 July 1989): 24.

Greenlaw, Lavinia. "The Owl's Story," *Times Literary Supplement* (16 February 1996): B13.

Kakutani, Michiko. "Sisters Looking for Ghosts in China," *New York Times* (17 November 1995): B13.

Koenig, Rhoda. "Nanking Pluck," *New York* (17 June 1991): 83.

Kramer, Barbara. *Amy Tan, Author of* The Joy Luck Club. Springfield, NJ: Enslow, 1996.

Ling, Amy, ed. *Between Worlds: Women Writers of Chinese Ancestry.* New York: Pergamon Press, 1990.

Lipson, Eden Ross. "The Wicked English-Speaking Daughter," *New York Times Book Review* (19 March 1989): 3.

Lyall, Sarah. "A Writer Knows that Spirits Dwell Beyond Her Pages," *New York Times* (29 December 1995): B1.

———. "In the Country of the Spirits: At Home with Writer Amy Tan," *New York Times* (28 December 1995): B1.

Mandell, Johathan. *New York Newsday* (15 July 1991): II, 46.

Merina, Anita. "Joy, Luck, and Lirarture," *NEA Today* 10, no. 3 (October 1991): 9.

Messud, Claire. "Ghost Story," *New York Times Book Review* (29 October 1995): 11.

Mitchell, David Thomas. *Conjured Communities: The Multiperspectival Novels of Amy Tan, Toni Morrison, Julia Alvares, Louise Erdrich, and Christina Garcia. DAI* 54, no. 1 (May 1994): 9409768.

Nurse, Donna. "House of the Spirits," *MacLean's* (6 November 1995): p. 85.

Ong, Caroline. "Re-Writing the Old Wives Tales," *Times Literary Supplement* (5 July 1991): 20.

——— . "Roots Relations," *Times Literary Supplement* (29 December 1989): 1447.

Paik, Felicia. *Ms. Magazine* (November–December 1995): 88.

Pavey, Ruth. "Spirit Levels," *New Statesman & Society* (16 February 1996): 38.

Peter, Nelson, and Peter Freundlich. "Women We Love: Nine Who Knock Us Out," *Esquire* (August 1989): 86.

Pollard, D.E. "Much Ado About Identity," *Far Eastern Economic Review* (27 July 1989): 41.

Reid, E. Shelley. *The Compound I: Narrative and Identity in the Novels of Toni Morrison, Louise Erdrich, and Amy Tan. DAI* 55, no. 11 (May 1995): 9509148.

Riordan, James. *Times Educational Supplement* (5 February 1993): R10. (*The Moon Lady*)

Roback, Diane, and Shannon Maughan. "Fall 1992 Children's Books," *Publisher's Weekly* (20 July 1992): 35.

Ryan, Marya Mae. *Gender and Community: Womanist and Feminist Perspectives in the Fiction of Toni Morrison, Amy Tan, Sandra Cisneros, and Louise Erdrich. DAI* 56, no. 9 (March 1996): 9543711.

Schecter, Ellen. "*The Moon Lady*," *New York Times Book Review* (8 November 1992): 31.

Scott, Margaret. "California Chinoiserie," *Far Eastern Economic Review* (30 May 1996): 37.

Shapiro, Laura. "Ghost Story," *Newsweek* (6 November 1995): 91.

———. "The Generation Gap in Chinatown," *Newsweek* (27 September 1993): 70.

———. *"The Kitchen God's Wife,"* *Newsweek* (24 June 1991): 63.

Shen, Gloria. "Born of a Stranger: Mother-Daughter Relationships and Storytelling in Amy Tan's *The Joy Luck Club,"* *International Women's Writing: New Landscapes of Identity.* Ed. Anne E. Brown and Marjanne E. Gooze. Westport, CT: Greenwood Press, 1995.

Simpson, Janice C., and Pico Iyer. "Fresh Voices Above the Noisy Din; New Works by Four Chinese-American Writers Splendidly Illustrate the Frustrations, Humor, and Eternal Wonder of the Immigrant's Life," *Time* (3 June 1991): 66

Skow, John. "Tiger Ladies," *Time* (27 March 1989): 98.

Smorada, Claudia Kovach. "Side-Stepping Death: Ethnic Identity, Contradiction, and the Mother(land) in Amy Tan's Novels," *Fu Jen Studies: Literature & Linguistics* 24 (1991): 31–45.

Sterritt, David. *"The Joy Luck Club,"* *Christian Science Monitor* (16 September 1993): 11.

Tan, Amy. "Amy Tan," *Writers Dreaming.* Ed. Naomi Epel. New York: Carol Southern Books, 1993.

———. "Angst and the Second Novel," *Publisher's Weekly* (5 April 1991): 4.

———. "Lost Lives of Women," *Life* 14, no. 4 (1 April 1991): 90–91.

"Tan, Amy," *Current Biography* 53, no. 2 (February 1992): 55.

Wong, Sau-Ling Cynthia. "'Sugar Sisterhood': Situating the Amy Tan Phenomenon," *The Ethnic Canon: Histories, Institutions, and Interventions.* Minneapolis: University of Minnesota Press, 1995. 174–210.

Woo, Elaine. *Los Angeles Times* (12 March 1989): VI, 14.

Young, Pamela. "Mother with a Past: The Family Album Inspires a Gifted Writer," *MacLean's* (15 July 1991): 47.

Acknowledgments

"Theorizing Ethnicity and Subjectivity: Maxine Hong Kingston's *Tripmaster Monkey* and Amy Tan's *The Joy Luck Club*" by Malini Johar Schueller from *Genders* 15 (Winter 1992): pp. 72–84. Copyright © 1992 by the University of Texas Press.

"Generational Differences and the Diaspora in *The Joy Luck Club*" by Walter Shear from *Critique* 34, no. 3 (Spring 1993). Reprinted with permission of the Helen Dwight Reid Educational Foundation. Published by Heldref Publications, 1319 Eighteenth Street, N.W., Washington D.C., 20036-1802. © 1993.

"Daughter-Text/Mother-Text: Matrilineage in Amy Tan's *Joy Luck Club*" by Marina Heung is a revised version of an article originally published in *Feminist Studies* 19, no. 3 (Fall 1993): 597–616. © 1993 Feminist Studies, Inc. Reprinted by permission of Feminist Studies, Inc.

"Memory and the Ethnic Self: Reading Amy Tan's *The Joy Luck Club*" by Ben Xu from *MELUS* Vol. 19, No. 1 (Spring 1994): pp. 3–19. Copyright © 1994 by the Society for the Study of Multi-Ethnic Literature of the U.S.

"'Only Two Kinds of Daughters': Inter-Monologue Dialogicity in *The Joy Luck Club*" by Stephen Souris from *MELUS* Vol. 19, No. 2 (Summer 1994): pp. 99–123. Copyright © 1994 by the Society for the Study of Multi-Ethnic Literature of the U.S.

"Chinese American Women, Language, and Moving Subjectivity" by Victoria Chen from *Women & Language* Vol. 18, No. 1 (Spring 1995): pp. 3–7. Copyright © 1995 by *Women & Language*.

"The Spirit Within: An Interview with Amy Tan" first appeared in *Salon* at http://www.Salon.com. An online version remains in the Salon archives. © 1995 *Salon*. Reprinted with permission.

"Swan-Feather Mothers and Coca-Cola Daughters: Teaching Amy Tan's *The Joy Luck Club*" by Wendy Ho from *Teaching American Ethnic Literatures; Nineteen Essays*, ed. John R. Maitino and David R. Peck. Copyright © 1996 by the University of New Mexico Press.

"*The Hundred Secret Senses*" by E. D. Huntley from *Amy Tan: A Critical Companion* by E. D. Huntley. Copyright © 1998 by E. D. Huntley.

"The Semiotics of China Narratives in the Con/texts of Maxine Hong Kingston and Amy Tan" by Yuan Yuan from *Critique* Vol. 40, No. 3 (Spring 1999): pp. 292–300. Copyright © 1999 by the Society for the Study of Multi-Ethnic Literature of the U.S.

Index